PERSPECTIVES ON COMMUNITIES:
A COMMUNITY ECONOMIC DEVELOPMENT ROUNDTABLE

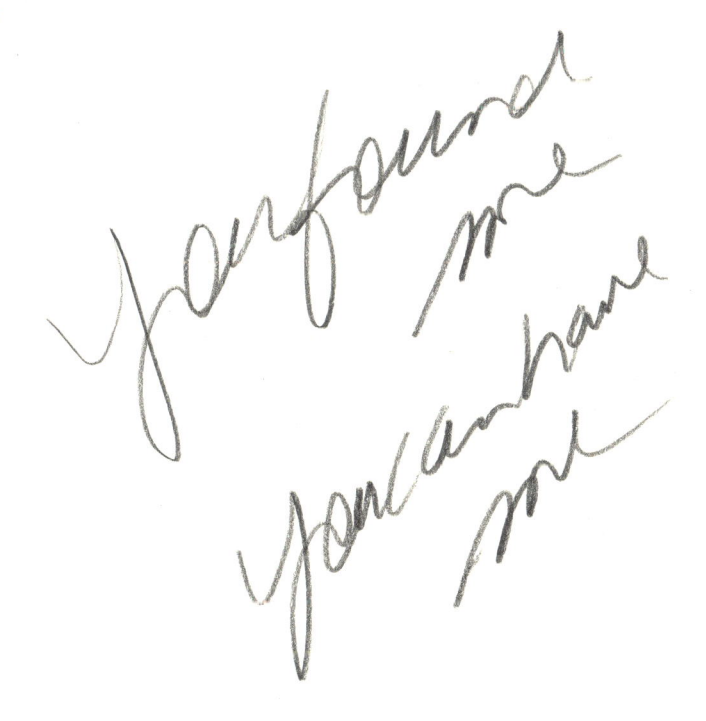

Gertrude Anne MacIntyre, Editor

UCCB Press

Sydney, Nova Scotia

CANADA

Copyright Gertrude Anne MacIntyre 1998.

All rights reserved. No part of this work may be reproduced or used in any form or by any means, electronic or mechanical, including photocopying, recording, or any information storage or retrieval system, without the prior written permission of the publisher.

The University College of Cape Breton Press acknowledges the support received of the Canada Council for the Arts for our publishing program.

Cover design by Ryan Astle, Goose Lane Editions
Front cover illustration, Barry Gabriel

Book design by Gail MacEachern
Printed and bound in Canada by City Printers, Sydney, NS.
Edited by Gertrude Anne MacIntyre

Canadian Cataloguing in Publication Data

Main entry under title

  Perspectives on communities
  ISBN 0-920336-57-4

1. Community development -- Nova Scotia -- Cape Breton Island. 2. Economic development projects -- Nova Scotia -- Cape Breton Island. I. MacIntyre, Gertrude Anne

HC117.N8P47 1998   338.9716'9   C98-950121-3

UCCB Press
Box 5300
Sydney, Nova Scotia
B1P 6L2
CANADA

TABLE OF CONTENTS

Preface 5
    Jacquelyn Thayer Scott

Introduction 9
    Gertrude Anne MacIntyre

PART 1
FOUNDATIONAL CONCEPTS IN COMMUNITY ECONOMIC DEVELOPMENT

Chapter 1 17
    The University and Community Development
    Gertrude Anne MacIntyre

Chapter 2 43
    The Community Business Corporation:
    La Empresa Social
    Greg MacLeod

Chapter 3 67
    Structural Considerations in the Creation of a
    Not-For-Profit Corporation
    Gary Corsano

PART 2
EMPIRICAL CASES IN COMMUNITY ECONOMIC DEVELOPMENT

Chapter 4 79
    New Dawn Enterprises Limited:
    A Community Economic Development Experiment
    Rankin MacSween

Chapter 5 91
    Financing Ventures in a Depleted Community
    Harvey Johnstone

Chapter 6 105
    The Mira Pasture Co-operative
    Charles MacDonald

Chapter 7 117
    The Survival of a Small Community
        Karen Malcolm
Chapter 8 135
    Enterprise Cape Breton Corporation:
    Where Top Down Meets Bottom Up
        Keith Brown

PART 3
TECHNOLOGY AND COMMUNITY ECONOMIC DEVELOPMENT

Chapter 9 159
    Information and Communications Technology and
    Local Economic Development
        Michael Gurstein
Chapter 10 183
    Community Economic Development and Persons
    with Disabilities: A Case Study and Critical Issues
    for Organization
        Scott MacAulay

PART 4
RESEARCH AND DEVELOPMENT IN COMMUNITY ECONOMIC DEVELOPMENT

Chapter 11 201
    Through A Glass Darkly: Looking for CED
        Constance P. deRoche
Chapter 12 225
    An Ear to the Ground: Grassroots Concerns
    About Employment and Economic Development
        Angus MacIntyre
Chapter 13 239
    Marginality, Liminality and Local Development
        Jim Lotz

Biographies 257

Abstract 261

Bibliography 267

Preface

Fads come and go in the fashion world. One year, hemlines rise alarmingly above the knees and lapels are pencil-thin; the next, skirts swirl near our ankles and the width of lapels and ties widens like a beach at ebb tide. Twenty-five years after we consigned our favourite bell-bottoms to the memory chest, along with our old Eagles albums, bell-bottomed trousers (and the Eagles, a little worse for wear!) are back.

The marketplace of public ideas is just as changeable, and sometimes as fickle. Some of you who pick up this book will be eager to learn about this new trend toward community economic development, a departure from the major industrial development focus in public policy that characterized the last century. Others will be interested in how the concept might apply in a post-industrial, knowledge-based world, and will understand the history of the concept—and may even have been young practitioners of the art during the 1960s, when community development experienced a brief period of popularity in Canadian public policy circles.

Since last practiced widely in North America, a new word has been added to the concept: community *economic* development. The addition of "economic" is not without controversy, however. Many will argue that economic development arises out of a cohesive community understanding and socio-economic infrastructure. While acknowledging this, critics will point out that history and changing global markets have taught us that community ventures must have a harder business edge to utilize scarce resources effectively. In any case, as Dr. MacIntyre notes in her opening chapter, "Community development has always been a very fuzzy concept, and before people can act effectively, they must come to terms with the internal dynamics of communities (and their own being) and the nature of the world beyond their boundaries."

Why is the concept of community economic development again rising to the top of the public policy agenda? More cynical (if historically accurate) observers may note that governments turn to communities to solve their own problems only when all other, and more grandiose, schemes have failed. Sympathizers, like myself, might argue that the timing is right for additional reasons. As the transformation to a post-industrial age accelerates, increasingly we realize that the most important geo-political dimensions are no longer necessarily at national or artificially drawn sub-national levels. Interactions, markets and meaning are more often global or local. What happens in Moscow or Guatemala matters and impacts on my own economic and environmental survival, but my community in Cape Breton matters most to my social, cultural and spiritual being. How can I mesh the two: support myself and my family in a global marketplace, yet live a meaningful life, rooted in a people and place?

These are not easy questions to answer, especially in a world, which in contemporary times has over-emphasized the dominance of the competition paradigm. Competition is real and critical to survival and success; careful observation of nature—"red of tooth and claw"—reveals this truth. Yet co-operation strategies, equally important, are mistakenly seen among stone-age remnants, crocodiles, and packs of wild predators or domesticated farm animals. Community economic development offers a complex of values and practical strategies to balance the competition/co-operation continuum—a "commons" to generate, evaluate and implement new answers to questions both old and new. But, as in any journey, it helps to have a guide, and *Perspectives* is a very useful and stimulating one.

PREFACE

It is no accident that this volume is being published by UCCB Press, and that most of its contributors have a present or past connection to this innovative higher education institution. Dr. MacIntyre tells part of our institutional story in her opening chapter. However, the limits of space constrain any author's ability to capture the breadth and depth of what has happened, and continues to occur, here.

It is sufficient to say that the commitment to community at the University College of Cape Breton is profound and deeply rooted—reflected in our mandate and mission, our architecture, the high-quality and multi-disciplinary nature of our academic programmes, with their connection to experiential learning and community research. In short, what we do arises from our view that all knowledge is unified and interconnected, and has a purpose—whether to be transformed into wealth for economic survival, or for the sheer enjoyment and enlightenment of the human heart and spirit. Learning, then, is a shared journey, not an elite commodity.

Accordingly, I am happy to bring you to the point of turning the page and embarking on a next stage of learning with the authors herein, who share your goal to give individuals and their communities new ideas and tools with which to build their own sustainable future.

Cape Breton Island Jacquelyn Thayer Scott, Ph.D.
April, 1998 President & Vice-Chancellor
University College of Cape Breton

INTRODUCTION

Gertrude Anne MacIntyre

In 1990, the Economic Council of Canada issued a "statement" entitled, *From the Bottom Up: The Community-Economic Development Approach*. It noted that federal and provincial governments were spending $230 million a year on community development programmes in marginalized parts of Canada and among people outside the mainstream of society. The Council—which was abolished by the federal government shortly after this report appeared—pointed out that the rising interest in community-based development has come about because of the repeated failures of "top-down," government-funded, centralized efforts at regional development.

Community development has become the flavour of the decade in Canada—and in Europe, where the European Union has been promoting it for lagging and depressed regions and communities. As the end of the millennium approaches, it seems certain that community economic development will be seen as a sure and certain way of generating jobs and "saving" marginal communities from all the ills that afflict them. In 1997, the J. W. McConnell Family Foundation launched The Community Economic Development Technical Assistance Program (CEDTAP), a four year national initiative to promote high performance community economic development among local organizations and professionals across Canada. Communities will be able to secure funds for planning, technical assistance and training to meet the needs they identify. The aim of CEDTAP is to strengthen communities that are taking action to create and retain jobs, develop local enterprise, and enhance local self-reliance—especially communities and groups that have been economically and socially disadvantaged.

Cape Breton is one of Canada's economically and socially disadvantaged regions. In the past, outsiders for their own ends exploited its resources. In recent years, too many attempts by well-intentioned, but poorly informed agencies and individuals to stimulate the economy of Cape Breton have failed to create employment or stimulate economic development. Increasingly, as have people elsewhere in Canada, Cape Bretoners have begun to demand that they be partners in policies, plans and programmes aimed at bettering their lives. They have taken initiatives to ensure this by creating a large number of economic development ventures. Cape Breton has emerged as national—and world—leader in this field, a laboratory and testing ground for new ways of meeting human needs in human ways. Not all initiatives have been successful. Community development of any kind is risky, and must be viewed as a form of research and development in handling change in creative and effective ways through democratic processes. Throughout recent history, the University College of Cape Breton has acted as an anchor for community development ventures on the Island. Faculty members and their colleagues in the development field, local leaders, as well as government officials and volunteers from many fields have worked together to better the lives of Cape Bretoners. Others have sought to analyze what community economic development is all about, so that theory and practice can go hand in hand. Much has been learned about the right—and wrong—ways to initiate, encourage and sustain locally based ventures.

Cape Bretoners, as they move into the future, have begun to recover a lost part of their history, that time in the Depression Years of the Dirty Thirties when the Antigonish Movement flourished. It brought new hope to communities and individuals struggling to sustain themselves in harder times than our own. Under the leadership of two remarkable Cape Bretoners—Fathers Jimmy Tompkins and Moses Michael Coady—the people of the Island sought to become masters of their destiny. They succeeded, by building strong, locally controlled institutions—credit unions and co-operatives—and because of the efforts of hundreds of volunteers, who found that in encouraging community development, they became more fully alive.

Perspectives on Communities: A Community Economic Development Roundtable describes a new, people-oriented economy led by locally controlled economic development organizations and government agencies. It provides examples of practical applications of CED theory in successful, sustainable community ventures that have made a social and economic impact on the lives of ordinary citizens living in Cape Breton, a non-metropolitan region of Nova Scotia, and elsewhere. The new jobs created have been secure, and people have gained from them a sense of identity and purpose.

This book, a collection of essays from authors active in the field of community economic development, is divided into four sections: Foundational Concepts in Community Economic Development, Empirical Cases in Community Economic Development, Technology and Community Economic Development, and Research and Development in Community Economic Development.

Section one is a theoretical perspective. Gertrude Anne MacIntyre discusses education as the foundation of development. She outlines a role for the university as a mediating structure in community-based development, helping to give those involved in local ventures some historical perspective and an understanding of the forces and factors that might influence their activities. Greg MacLeod proposes a conceptualization of the "community business corporation" as a composite of the co-operative tradition and the modern multi-national. He uses select examples from Mondragon, Spain, and New Dawn in Cape Breton to test his theory.

Gary Corsano outlines some of the legal ramifications inherent in community development corporations, while reflecting on the CED issues of governance and decision-making within them.

In section two, five concrete cases in community economic development in Cape Breton are explored: New Dawn Enterprises Limited, BCA Holdings Limited, The Mira Pasture Co-op, Development Isle Madame (DIMA), and a government agency, Enterprise Cape Breton Corporation. Rankin MacSween draws on the history and culture of Cape Breton to provide the context for New Dawn Enterprises, Canada's oldest community development corporation. He points out that New Dawn is a "futuristic instrument," part of an international movement that may restructure our communities in the 21st century. Harvey Johnstone examines a different kind of business, BCA Holdings (Banking Community Assets), an experimental, community venture-finance company. BCA is a not-for-profit organization. But like a profit-driven venture, it must operate on sound economic principles to manage and reduce risk. Any profits generated by BCA are used for further community development projects. Charles MacDonald's chapter on the Mira Pasture Co-op provides an example of two basic principles of CED: collaboration and "sweat equity." The beginnings of the Mira Pasture Co-op, like those of New Dawn, go back to the mid-1970s, when many new initiatives were undertaken to address the economic and social problems facing Cape Breton. While New Dawn started in an urban environment, the city of Sydney, the Co-op had its roots in rural Cape Breton, and tackled the problem in the decline of agriculture. Karen Malcolm presents the story of Development Isle Madame Association. Some residents of Isle Madame, Cape Breton, were determined to remain in their community when the mainstay of their economy, the fishing industry, shut down. In the midst of this economic crisis, the community banded together to form DIMA, a grassroots organization whose mandate was to find alternative ways to develop their community. The process that DIMA used is a model for community-based planning and action. The final essay in this section demonstrates the contribution of a government agency, Enterprise Cape Breton Corporation, to the Cape Breton community. Keith Brown presents research on the genesis and development of ECBC over the past 30 years. Using tourism and aquaculture as examples, he shows how its policies have been supportive of CED initiatives on the Island.

Technology as a resource for CED is discussed in section three of *Perspectives*. In a post-industrial society, technology can work against or for marginalized societies. Automation and centralization can mean the loss of jobs and decline of the non-metropolitan areas, but because technology is place-neutral, it can flourish in non-metropolitan areas and thus enable isolated areas to play leading roles in the information economy. The chapter by Michael Gurstein provides a broad framework for understanding the role of Information and Communications Technology (ICT) in local community development. Scott MacAulay provides some critical reflection on the broader questions technology raises for local community economic development. The case he presents is unique. The community group involved is a sector of our population traditionally forgotten by mainstream CED—"persons with disabilities." MacAulay highlights many accepted elements of successful CED projects, including the active participation of a community group, and strong leadership and partnerships with both private- and public-sector representatives.

The fourth section of *Perspectives* pursues research and further reflections on CED. Constance deRoche queries the meaning of CED to get at issues such as local ownership and loci of control. She asks how ordinary people, with no personal power or personal control of extraordinary resources, cope within the current global economic restructuring. Angus MacIntyre asks timely questions about jobs. Everyone wants a job, but what kind of job is desirable? His informal research project signals the need for a more extensive, formal investigation in this area. The section concludes with a chapter by Jim Lotz who relates the concepts of liminality and community. He discusses the tension created when old ways of thinking about development (government-sponsored and -supported) conflict with the new responsibilities now being placed on communities (to take care of themselves). As he points out, when more and more people in marginal areas are suspended in this state of limbo, we have to identify neutral ground where concerned citizens and government officials can meet and interact in mutually beneficial ways.

Cape Breton is small enough to tackle problems in human ways, and large enough that generalizations from what has happened here can be made, that might be useful to others in Canada and elsewhere in the world who hang between a dismal past and the promise of a brighter future. As we have learned in Cape Breton, community development touches people at their deepest levels as they seek to live what Moses Coady called "the full and abundant life." In a world dominated by multinational corporations and large domestic entities, at a time when so many of our leaders seem to have lost their way, the essential moral, spiritual and ethical concerns that motivate those who engage in community development offer a way of assuaging the many ills that affect individuals and communities, while they offer an avenue of hope into an uncertain future.

PART 1

FOUNDATIONAL CONCEPTS IN COMMUNITY ECONOMIC DEVELOPMENT

1

THE UNIVERSITY AND COMMUNITY DEVELOPMENT
GERTRUDE ANNE MACINTYRE

Community development has often been a child of hard times. This is one reason for its growing popularity among governments as a way of handling increasing expectations in a time of limited resources. Through history, a new concept of community has emerged out of crisis whenever an old order declined and a new one was born. Saint Augustine wrote *The City of God* as barbarians besieged Rome. Monasteries developed as the Roman Empire declined and Europe was plunged into darkness. Sir Thomas More wrote *Utopia* in 1516, as Henry VIII extended his power and set about "privatizing" the monasteries and while the wealthy extended their holdings at the expense of the poor.

Idealistic efforts at creating new forms of community are often dismissed as "utopian." Those who say so, however, surely have not read More's work. His ideal community bears a strong resemblance to the world of Orwell's *1984*. These days, as governments struggle to adapt to change, many people feel they are hanging in limbo between utopia and dystopia, between an ideal world of the imagination and its polar opposite.

Community development has often been promoted as a simple grassroots, bottom-up approach to social change, a way of empowering the powerless, of confronting governments about their inadequacies, of radicalizing the marginalized. Academics have discussed community development on theoretical planes having no relation to reality. The editors of *Community Development in America* titled their introductory chapter "In Search of Community Development."[1] In it, they gave nineteen definitions of community development, calling it variously a process, a method, a programme, a movement. In recent years, community development has even been described as a paradigm, a favourite word to describe something new. While useful, this analytical approach to community development ignores the fact that social action at the local level can be a process that is part of a programme, using methods that help people to help themselves. As those involved make contact with worlds beyond their boundaries, they recognize that they are involved in a social movement.

Efforts to define community development, taking up as they do immense amounts of time, divert attention from the key concern in this field: what kinds of organizations are most effective in actually doing community development.

Canada has seen a wide variety of efforts to set up and run community development projects. This chapter looks at the role that universities can play in community development. Its main focus is on the Island of Cape Breton, Nova Scotia, where the University College of Cape Breton (UCCB) has been a significant player. The history of the Island is sketched as the context for discussing the connection between our University and community development initiatives. And the role of UCCB's Community Economic Development (CED) Institute is highlighted to demonstrate how a university can successfully provide an open, communal space, "part of the common," for people involved in community development.

Here, they can exchange ideas, information and experience; develop new projects; try experiments in social change, and spin off new ventures.

Increasingly, Canadian universities are urged to serve their communities, rather than to copy the British "Town and Gown" model of universities. In the United States, early land-grant universities were required to serve local communities. They developed extension departments, and their faculty received advancement for public service. In Canada, as in Britain, however, promotion and prestige in academic bodies came from publishing and research; little attention was paid to teaching. In fact, community service has never been considered a vital part of university life in Canada, tending instead to be relegated to the margins of our academic institutions.[2]

Lotz[3] has examined two contrasting cases of university involvement in community development in Canada. The University of Alberta came into being in 1890, three years after the province became a separate political entity. Henry Marshall Tory, the University's first president, had to convince the politicians and the people of the pioneer province that the University could play a useful role in provincial life. He worked hard to take education to Albertans wherever they lived. Faculty members went into the countryside, lecturing on topics ranging from Shakespeare to sewage treatment. In 1912, Edward Ottewell became secretary of the University's extension department. He trundled around the province in an old car with a travelling library and slides (to supplement the public lectures) on a host of topics such as women's suffrage and immigration. He also distributed plays suitable for amateur theatrical productions, and after the war, theatre became a powerful force for generating community cohesion in many parts of Alberta as local people struggled to survive during the Great Depression. These productions provided not only entertainment, but also a way for community groups to work together creatively.

In the affluent years after the Second World War, however, another university venture in community development began, this time in Saskatchewan, but it ultimately failed to sustain itself. In 1952, as urbanization accelerated, the Saskatchewan government launched a Royal Commission on Agriculture. The Commission reported to the provincial government in 1956. In the following year, its director headed up the Centre for Community Studies at the University of Saskatchewan. The Centre received government funding and a threefold mandate: to study the development of Saskatchewan communities, to serve organizations in community development, and to offer in-service training for professionals in the field. The Centre soon began to experience tensions between its research activities and those dedicated to generating grassroots action. While the Centre did a great deal of valuable pioneering work, it ran into trouble when the government changed in 1964. The staff tried to integrate the institution's operations into University life, but its practical bent upset the traditionalists who controlled the University of Saskatchewan. The Centre slowly faded out of existence after it moved off the University campus in 1965. As one commentator put it, the concept of community development had become a euphemism for "doing little things in little places."[4]

Significant social change involves shifts in economic, social and political structures, including rearrangements in role patterns and relationships between and within those structures. Community development looks attractive to governments, especially in times of fiscal restraint, because it costs little and seems like an effective way of stimulating self-help at the local level and taking some of the weight off line agencies. As Davies puts it:

> "It was difficult for the Centre's community developers to face up to the fact that substantial local development would mean a large

> scale investment—inevitably from outside sources—either in the area's underdeveloped resources, or else in the relocation and rehabilitation of under-employed local populations."[5]

Government's tendency to see community development as a simple way of solving complex problems emerges in the story of one effort to improve life for the Indian and Métis (people of French and Indigenous ancestry) in Manitoba. A study of these people in 1956-59 revealed the miserable conditions under which they lived. The report recommended a community development programme "to help people of Indian ancestry to solve their own problems," adding that "it might be judged too idealistic were it not that there are already such programs operating successfully in different parts of the world."[6] The report envisaged that community development workers would win the confidence of local people, helping them to identify their needs, preparing them for action, assisting them in using local resources, co-ordinating the work of other government services, and identifying the readiness of white residents to work with them. The Manitoba government set up a Community Development Branch in the Department of Welfare. Jean Lagassé, a Métis social worker, hired to head it, understood what community development meant, and set down his ideas on paper, identifying as its fundamental principles:

> • That all people, no matter how unambitious they may appear, have a desire to better themselves.
>
> • That the difficulties preventing the fulfillment of people's needs are too great for the resources that they have.
>
> • That all groups can do something to help themselves when given an opportunity to do so on their own terms.

> • That in order to achieve lasting change it is necessary to influence simultaneously various aspects of human behavior.[7]

Lagassé saw community development workers as facilitators, enablers, organizers and animators, working with Native people at their point of need. He recognized that in many communities, outsiders from government and other large organizations held most of the power. Manitoba's community development programme attracted idealistic young people, one of whom, when he arrived on a reserve was asked, "What are you going to do for us?" His reply: "I'm here to find out what you can do for yourselves."

After Lagassé left his position in 1963, the Manitoba programme slowly lost steam. It lost the high degree of autonomy it had had and, eventually vanished into the bureaucracy of the Department of Welfare. Meanwhile, the Manitoba government outlined vast northern development schemes to the Indian and Métis peoples, claiming they would employ Natives and create a better life for them.

The impact of community development workers did not fade from memory as Native people sought greater control over their destinies. It is more than coincidence that the Indians of Manitoba were the first to negotiate a self-government agreement with the federal government.

In reviewing the history of community development in Canada, two strong themes emerge: the importance of leaders in stimulating self-help, mutual aid and community initiative at critical times in the country's history; and the persistence of memory—the impact that the past has on the present. These factors have played a significant role in the resurgence of interest in community development in Nova Scotia, especially in Cape Breton.

Schratz and Walker point out the four dimensions of human existence around which community development and any change efforts revolve.[8] Closeness, distance, continuity and change are represented in their book as four arms of a cross each pulling in a different direction. Closeness requires familiarity, longing for love, social contact, harmony and commitment. Distance involves a quest for difference, individualism, freedom and autonomy. The tensions in meeting these two opposing demands are played out in time and space in communities. Continuity depends on order, planning, rules, power arrangements and control. Change focuses on the lure of the unknown, the new, escapes from the familiar, alteration to established patterns and spontaneity. The tension between these two thrusts has to be managed at the community, regional, and national levels.

Closeness and distance, continuity and change are not polar opposites. The terms in each pair represent opposite ends of a spectrum, while human need lies within each range. Everyone needs close relationships with others to flourish, as well as time alone. Everyone seeks stability and security, but also opportunities for change. Governments direct most of their efforts at ensuring stability and security for their peoples, despite their rhetoric about change and how wonderful it is. The private sector stresses the need for change, offering new products, goods and services to lure consumers. Community development seeks to balance contrasting needs for stability and security and those focused on change. Thus, the process always has a highly ambiguous feel to it. Neither the government nor the private sector is well suited to initiating and managing community development.

Cape Breton has emerged as a classic example of the failure of governments to improve life in ways that residents feel to be compatible with their values. The Island lies at the eastern tip of Nova Scotia, a 6,500-square-kilometre landmass with a population of about 160,000 people. It played a significant role in European and North American history: the rich fisheries attracted French and English ships, making Nova Scotia a battlefield between the two countries. In 1713, Cape

Breton (then *Isle Royale*) became the key to France's retention of Canada (New France). Located strategically near the mouth of the St. Lawrence River, the Island could control movement in this part of North America. In 1713, under the Treaty of Utrecht, the French, who began to build a huge fortress at Louisbourg (formerly English Harbour), retained *Isle Royale*. The Fortress became the first of the many huge and expensive follies to dot the landscape of Nova Scotia. Like so many other megaprojects, Fortress of Louisbourg had some serious flaws. Designed in the tradition of French fortresses, its thick wall began to crumble under the impact of salt air and frost. And because Louis XV had difficulty finding guns for his other continental wars, only 79 of the 148 pieces of artillery planned for the Fortress were actually installed. What is more, the garrison consisted of Swiss mercenaries, an expensive form of human resources. Stuck in fog, wet, and short of food in a place that smelled heavily of fish, the soldiers mutinied in December 1744 and took over the town.

When war broke out between France and Britain, New England colonists besieged and captured the fortress in 1745. (Historians have called Louisbourg the cradle of the United States.) In 1748, the British handed the Fortress back to the French. For the New Englanders, all their effort and suffering had been for nothing.

In 1758, Louisbourg was again besieged and taken. At the Treaty of Paris, *Isle Royale* became a British possession and was renamed Cape Breton Island. Under British colonial rule, the people of the Island soon learned how their interests could be subordinated to those of the ruling power.

The British did not allow coal mining on the Island because it would compete with their own exports of coal. This did not prevent Cape Bretoners from opening and working bootleg mines. In fact, Cape Bretoners' notorious resistance to local authority is echoed in the words of the last governor of the colony, who denounced them as a "set of deceitful, unprincipled aliens, imbued with the Yankee qualities of the refuse of three kingdoms."[9] Large-scale coal mining on Cape Breton began because of royal financial problems. The Duke of York, brother of King George IV, held a lease on all mineral wealth of Nova Scotia. When he began to run short of money, he sold the mine fields to his jewelers, Messrs. Rundell, Bridge and Rundell. They formed the General Mining Association and began to mine coal in Cape Breton and Inverness Counties, where coal provided employment for those the land could not sustain. Displaced Scots had flooded into Cape Breton during the 19th century, many settling on marginal land. When their small farms could not sustain their offspring, they moved to the mining towns to work. In 1893, a Boston financier, Henry Melville Whitney, consolidated a number of collieries and created the Dominion Coal Company. It produced more coal than he could use in the New England market, so he opened a steel mill in Sydney in 1901. Another company erected a steel mill nearby.

Conditions in the coal and steel towns were abysmal. Company stores, known as "pluck-me stores," sold miners their tools and food for their families. As the only stores in town, they charged exorbitant rates, keeping most of their customers in lifelong debt. Company-owned houses provided minimal shelter and deteriorated through the years. The mines and steel mills flourished during the First World War, but the years after 1918 were marked by cuts in wages, short hours and increasing militancy among the workers. Life in rural communities became increasingly difficult as well. Somehow people managed to sustain themselves, to raise families, relish simple joys and keep alive the hope of a better life.

Then in 1926 and 1927, a crisis occurred in the fishing industry. Favourable weather allowed offshore steam trawlers to land large catches and depress the price of fish. Fishermen at Canso, on the southeastern tip of the Nova Scotia mainland, gathered on the wharf on July 1, 1927 to complain that they had nothing to celebrate on the 60th anniversary of

Canadian Confederation. Their parish priest asked them what they were going to do about their plight. That priest was Father Jimmy Tompkins.[10] Years earlier, as vice-president of Saint Francis Xavier University, he had urged the University to take knowledge to the people, instead of educating only the brightest young men for jobs elsewhere. For Father Tompkins, adult education was the most effective way to create economic and social development in eastern Nova Scotia. Father Jimmy's radicalism, his promotion of university integration in Nova Scotia, upset the Catholic hierarchy so much that they banished him to Canso. There he began to put his ideas about adult education into action. In the fishing crisis of 1926-27, he encouraged local fishermen to co-operate to obtain a better price for their catch and to buy what they needed more cheaply.

Father Jimmy Tompkins was a leader of the Catholic social action venture that became known as the Antigonish Movement, and that movement was itself rooted in the encyclical, *Rerum Novarum,* issued by Pope Leo XIII on May 15, 1891. To counter the growing nationalism in Europe and the bureaucratization of society, the encyclical defended the rights of the family and private property against the encroachments of the state. It stressed that "labour is not a commodity," and advocated legislation to encourage the formation of trade unions and co-operative ventures. The encyclical gave priests in Nova Scotia a mandate for action. Activist priests worked with farmers to help them buy supplies and market their products. And the fisheries crisis and protests at Canso resulted in the formation of a Royal Commission on the Maritime Provinces and the Magdalen Islands. The report, released in May, 1928, painted a grim picture of idle men and idle boats in depressed communities. And it recommended the formation of co-operatives to give fishermen more power over their destinies. The federal government hired Father Moses Coady, Father Jimmy's cousin, to organize the fishermen. Thus began what is now known as the Antigonish Movement.

Co-operatives were not new in Nova Scotia. Immigrant miners had formed one in Stellarton in 1861. The genius of Coady and his people at the Extension Department at St. Francis Xavier University lay in their application of adult education to the formation of credit unions and co-operatives. Using a wide range of media, the Extension field staff urged people in small communities to "Listen. Study. Discuss. Act."

The 1930s, a time of economic depression in the rest of Canada, became a shining moment for Nova Scotia. People came from all over the world to learn from Coady and his followers. The Antigonish Movement reached its peak just before the Second World War, with 19,600 people studying self-help in 2,265 study groups. When Father Tompkins was transferred to Reserve Mines in Cape Breton in 1935, he urged local miners to build their own homes. They did so and called their village Tompkinsville. Father Jimmy also started a library. Unlike Father Coady, who offered simple, direct recipes for tackling economic problems.[11] Father Jimmy encouraged local people to read widely and to see their problems in national and international context, perhaps because of his own university-based experience. Exiled from the university, he took higher learning beyond campus borders. Amidst the postwar affluence, however, the lessons of the Antigonish Movement were forgotten.

In retrospect, the forces that generated this remarkable venture in community economic development emerge clearly. A hierarchical structure, the Catholic Church, under the pressures of change in Europe, found a spokesman in a broad-minded Pope. His encyclical gave priests and their bishops a mandate for social action. A few of them, like Father Jimmy, acted upon these new ideas and championed adult education. In the Catholic tradition, priests tended to be sent to parishes for long periods so that they might offer stable support to their communities. This worked well for Father Jimmy, who became the visionary of the Antigonish Movement. Meanwhile, at the Extension Department, Coady brought together a group of dedicated people to help those in rural communities set up study clubs, as a first step toward credit unions and co-operatives. The provincial and federal governments backed the move towards co-operation and gave some support. Much of the funding for the Extension Department at St. Francis Xavier in Antigonish came, however, from the Carnegie Corporation. Thus Coady and his people had a financial backer whose activities could not be hampered by the petty politics of the day. The Extension Department was very effective, despite not because of, University support. The independent financial and moral support given Tompkins by officials at the Carnegie Corporation played a significant role in the success of the Antigonish Movement. Secure funding meant that time would not have to be spent searching for the financial means to support their activities, and it allowed them greater autonomy.

After 1945, the economy of Cape Breton began to decline. The owners of the coal mines and steel mills invested little new capital in them, allowing them to deteriorate. Productivity declined, competition grew, and oil replaced coal as the main industrial and domestic fuel. As coal mines closed, the federal government set up a Royal Commission to study the problems of the industry. The Commission concluded that mining had no future. In 1967, the federal government set up the Cape Breton Development Corporation (DEVCO) to rationalize the coal industry and to generate alternate employment on the Island. DEVCO operated the remaining coal mines and encouraged outsiders to open factories. A string of "investors" took government money and tax breaks, then closed up shop and left. Two heavy-water plants built by the government closed when a market for their product failed to develop.

In 1967, the British owners of the steel plant in Sydney announced that they would close it in the following year. The provincial government set up a crown corporation, Sydney

Steel Corporation (SYSCO), and bought the plant. Since then, the government has spent about $2 billion to try to make the venture profitable. In 1995, SYSCO entered into a joint venture with Chinese entrepreneurs to run the mill. That plan failed, and in 1998, the intent is to sell the plant to the Mexicans. Since its inception thirty years ago, DEVCO has absorbed about $1 billion in public funds, and now simply operates the remaining coal mines.

The high cost of public support for resource industries has become familiar throughout marginal areas of the world. It helps explain government's obsession currently with community economic development and their talk of partnerships between communities and governments.

Government's failure to ameliorate the problems of poverty in ways acceptable to its victims has led to an upsurge in local initiatives. In the 1970s, a small group of people on Cape Breton led by Father Greg MacLeod, a charismatic priest and philosophy professor at the University College of Cape Breton (UCCB), began to revive the tradition of the Antigonish Movement. They used its approach to give local people more power over their social and economic destinies.

Watching with some bewilderment various government efforts to stimulate economic development, MacLeod's group borrowed the American idea of a community development corporation. Community development corporations—operated by, for and with local residents—had started business ventures, improved housing and provided services in disadvantaged parts of the United States.

The first community development corporation in Canada, New Dawn Enterprises, started in 1973 in response to local need. A group of people in Sydney borrowed money, bought a rundown building and fixed it up with grant money and volunteer labour. They began the process of supporting new ventures and building affordable housing. They also secured services like dentistry for Sydney. New Dawn now has 100 employees, an annual payroll of almost $2 million and assets of $20 million. That business serve a social purpose is the cornerstone to their activities, not that business simply generate profit. New Dawn is now self-sustaining, relying on dedicated volunteers to keep it going. Those involved have learned how to work co-operatively with government agencies.

Community development is not spontaneous. It requires a sophisticated understanding at senior levels in government and the private sector to flourish. New Dawn has emerged as a research and development experiment in social and economic change and in local empowerment. It has not always succeeded. A diaper service lost $150,000 before being terminated. But New Dawn has freely admitted and publicized its failures, and it has served as a model for a number of other community development corporations in Cape Breton and elsewhere in Canada.

Continuing adult education in the tradition of the Antigonish Movement played a significant role in establishing New Dawn and in ensuring its survival. The faculty and staff at the University College of Cape Breton have provided administrative support, leadership, technical expertise, advocacy skills, resources and access to funding. And UCCB helped to found the Centre for Community Economic Development in Sydney in 1988 as a support facility for local ventures. When federal government funding for this Centre ended in 1993, the University re-established it on campus in 1995, as the Community Economic Development (CED) Institute.

Community development, in all of its various forms, is usually what people resort to when other approaches to change have failed. Thus it tends to be viewed in messianic terms, as the solution to all human ills. One problem in helping communities to acquire the skills they need to manage change is the initial need to determine "where a community is" at a given time. Communities are not simple, unitary entities; they are arenas of competing visions, demands, needs and priorities. A case in point is the community of Reserve Mines, Cape Breton.

In the late 1980s, members of the Reserve Mines Credit Union were instructed by their central office to amalgamate with another local branch of the credit union. (Reserve Mines, chartered in January 1933, was the first English-speaking credit union in Atlantic Canada.) Instead, the Reserve Mines members decided to take control over their own destinies and turned to Professor Greg MacLeod, then president of BCA Holdings, a community venture finance company, for technical and financial support. They dreamed of erecting their own credit union. And ingeniously, by cutting costs and using volunteer professionals for advice, they made the dream a reality. The new credit union secured tenants to help pay building maintenance costs. It created 25 new jobs, saved six more, and increased the range of services to the whole community. The memory of Father Jimmy Tompkins was one of the driving forces in this project: the parents of one of its key organizers had been part of the housing co-operative sixty years before, and by general agreement, the Credit Union members called their community economic development venture Tompkins Development Limited.

Community development often begins with one committed individual. Many times, it is a visionary who is a marginal member of a community. The Community Economic Development (CED) Institute serves as a place where such visionaries can discuss their ideas and receive a sympathetic hearing. This is a unique function. Many organizations and institutions in the community economic development field offer answers to problems. But the CED Institute can offer *a place where the focus is formulating the right questions* about community economic development.

The CED Institute, through its Advisory Board of UCCB faculty and community members, believes that *the process of development works best when local people control it and take primary responsibility for it.* The Institute performs several support functions in the community. It facilitates technology transfer from the University to the community level, providing a vehicle for getting the message of community economic development out to the communities. It provides technical advice to groups with ideas for community development, thus helping community groups find their own solutions to local problems, make basic decisions, and mobilize resources for their projects. The CED Institute offers community economic development training, policy advice and evaluation, organization and community strategic planning, and information about community consultative processes. One vital function of the CED Institute is promoting the exchange of information among those active in the field. To this end, the Institute provides workshops, conferences, newsletters and video presentations. It has also offered a variety of programmes since its inception. One example is the annual "Learning Vacation in CED," which attracts people from across North America for a week-long immersion in CED theory and its practical application in Cape Breton.

CED is widely promoted but there is a need for a better understanding of why it works, where it works, and which organizational forms are most effective. Currently, policy makers either treat CED as a panacea for all the ills of the world, or dismiss it as a marginal undertaking. In the past, community organizations have tended to hover between anarchy and bureaucracy. Yet much research exists about how modern management operates, research that could help build managerial capacity in communities. We need to know how to spot and support community and social entrepreneurs who have the knack for doing CED in its various forms.

The CED Institute is a vehicle for focusing some of UCCB's research effort on CED issues. For example, the Institute has planned a long-term, applied research study on the role public schools can play in CED. Working with UCCB's School of Business, it provided research and leadership in designing and implementing a Master of Business Administration in Community Economic Development. The MBA (CED) gives course participants the best information and ideas on CED, and asks them to contribute their ideas and experiences to enrich the learning of others. The CED Institute has also been helpful in identifying materials on CED suitable for publication by the UCCB Press, acting to control the quality of materials published on CED. This initiative helps to meet the growing need for reliable information in this field.

UCCB has a history of involvement in community development. The University/College had its genesis in Xavier College, founded in 1951 as a branch campus of St. Francis Xavier University in Cape Breton. In 1974, the College of Cape Breton united Xavier College with the Nova Scotia Eastern Institute of Technology (NSEIT), a vocational and technical college. The College's first degree was a Bachelor of Arts degree in Community Studies (BACS),

> "based on the teachings of John Dewey, Alfred North Whitehead, and Paulo Freire... (and)...was characterized by uniqueness and innovation in its approach to teaching and learning...rooted in the community, in the unity of knowledge, and the dignity of work."[12]

The backbone of the BACS degree is Problem-Centred Studies (PCS), which is concerned with the process of analyzing and exploring issues the groups themselves identify and wish to investigate:

> "...PCS 100 centres on critical thinking and analysis...problem-solving strategies, basic secondary research techniques...and decision making. PCS 200 groups turn their attention to primary research techniques and are encour-

aged to apply their skills in local communities. PCS 300 groups...undertake applied research for developing a community project."[13]

In 1982, the College of Cape Breton became the University College of Cape Breton, an independent institution whose mandate was personal, social, and economic development.[14] UCCB is newer than other universities in the province. Older, more elitist traditions have not dominated at UCCB. In fact, the province's established universities lobbied against competition. Their lobby succeeded: UCCB could not offer traditional degrees; all of its degrees must be innovative. This remains the case today. UCCB's first graduate programme, the Master of Business Administration in Community Economic Development, was designed to differ from all existing MBA degrees.

Foresight and alternative values helped UCCB to develop and survive; but external circumstances forced it to adapt as well. For example, UCCB's amalgamation with NSEIT was due to UCCB's late arrival on the university scene. Nova Scotia has an inordinate number of post-secondary institutions to support, and amalgamations, like that one were provincial cost-cutting measures.

UCCB now offers Bachelor degrees in Arts, Science, Business Administration and Technology, as well as in Community Studies, and it has a whole cadre of non-credit courses and services. These include an Extension and Community Affairs Department, a CAD-CAM Centre, a Geographical Information System Centre, a Chair in the Management of Technological Change, a Centre for International Studies, and various institutes such as the Tompkins and CED.

Through its diverse programmes and activities, UCCB has a profound impact on the development of the Cape Breton community. The faculty at the University started, fostered, and operated community economic development ventures under extremely difficult circumstances. Moreover, UCCB is a partner, with three levels of government, in the Cape Breton County Economic Development Authority (CBCEDA). And it encourages and rewards its faculty's applied research and technical assistance activities. The School of Business offers a unique Master of Business Administration degree in Community Economic Development, the first of its kind in Canada, as well as courses at the undergraduate level in CED. This school helped form a Tourism Policy Group to bring together key players in Nova Scotia and Cape Breton Tourism. In association with the Industrial Board of Trade, it assisted the Cape Breton Regional Municipality in a number of public and private initiatives like the privatization of the local airport in Sydney, and the establishment of Sydney's largest convention and recreation facility, Centre 200. UCCB staff has pioneered community-networking forums, such as the Technology Advisory Group (TAG), and they have led in organizing the Culture and Heritage Advisory Group (CHAG).

UCCB has shown commitment and leadership in its response to the needs identified by the community (and communities) it serves, mediating, facilitating and animating at the local level. It has functioned as a "mediating structure."

Berger and Neuhaus have pointed out a paradox of modern society: people demand more and more from government and the private sector while mistrusting them profoundly.[15] Everyone wants the benefits of the welfare state, without giving up personal freedom. Governments and large corporations, however, cannot give people a sense of identity and purpose beyond the job and the daily round of work. "Mediating structures" can. These are organizations that stand between individuals and larger entities of society. Community groups, volunteer organizations, and local societies are all mediating structures. Berger and Neuhaus discuss the role of four mediating structures: neighbourhoods, family, church and voluntary associations.

In *Active Partners: Education and Local Development*, I explored the way schools too can serve as mediating structures.[16] Such mediators help reconcile national and provincial policies and plans with local needs, offering a place to examine mutually beneficial initiatives. Thus policy formulation and planning, and their implementation by community agencies, can be harmonized and better use made of existing resources. As mediating structures, schools can be used more imaginatively to strengthen local economies and prepare young people for meaningful employment at home or elsewhere in the global village. They can bring together those concerned with education and economic and social development to discuss ways of bridging solitudes. UCCB has served as a mediating structure in the development of an education partnership with Cape Breton schools. For example, its entrepreneurship programme, which focuses upon developing self-confidence and entrepreneurial attitudes in young people to help them take control of their own future, recently won a national award—the "partnership Focus Award"—given by the Conference Board of Canada and other sponsor. And the CED Institute continues to search for new ways to strengthen its role as a mediating structure at local, provincial and national levels.

One function of mediating structures is to provide a reliable source of information for those who seek authentic knowledge about community development. Local leaders know how important information is to help them control and respond to change in their communities. In community development, as in so many other fields, there is no shortage of information. But as Gertrude Stein put it, "Everybody gets so much information all day long that they lose their common sense." The academic tendency to see information as flowing in only one direction hampers the role that wisdom, knowledge and the experience of local people can play as communities adapt and change. The CED Institute mediates knowledge and common sense by respecting the expertise born of the practical experience of ordinary people.

In the past three decades in Canada, so many community development ventures have arisen, flourished for a while, then vanished. Some teetered on the brink of dissolution all the time and ultimately descended into anarchy. Others became bureaucratized. In the 1960s, the emphasis in community economic development was a social concern—helping the poor and the marginalized to gain greater control over their lives. In the 1970s, the emphasis moved to public participation (usually directed at stopping social change rather than encouraging it) and interest group activity. Communities became divided, though talk about co-ordination increased. Beginning in the 1980s, as two recessions hit Canada, community economic development emerged as a panacea for poor communities, Indian reserves and other depressed areas. Now it is being touted as the answer to all economic problems, everywhere and anywhere, again.

The very word "community" has great appeal, especially to governments, in a time when the gaps between them and the people for whose destinies they are responsible continue to widen. Community policing, community health programmes, community involvement in recreation...the list goes on. In rationalizing their activities, agencies invoke so abstract a concept of community that it becomes invisible in their operations. The recent talk about "civil society" and communitarianism appears to ignore that lesson, however.

Governments and large corporations are the main determinants of what happens in society today. Governments are responsible for social control, while the private sector focuses on generating profits. Increasingly, ordinary citizens in liberal democracies feel powerless in dealing with either sector. However, these large bodies also contain men and women who are committed to community development, for whom involvement is a spiritual concern, not merely a means of delivering programmes and services.

Although universities in Canada are being forced to do more with less, individuals in them remain committed to serving their communities. The University College of Cape Breton has served as a mediating structure in community-based development, helping to link top-down and bottom-up efforts in local development. University participation in community development has helped to give those involved in local ventures an historical understanding of the forces that influence their activities. There is, of course, danger in community development always of stifling local initiatives, offering the wrong help and advice at the wrong time. Almost inevitably, new community development ventures fumble initially, not recognizing that they need help. And help is not always available. Increasingly, governments are withdrawing from communities, expecting residents to operate programmes on a volunteer basis; meanwhile, in this time of great uncertainty, the private sector keeps its eyes firmly fixed on the bottom line.

Canadian universities' three traditional roles of teaching, research and publication can be extended. The university can offer neutral ground where people concerned about CED can meet, talk, and exchange ideas and experiences. The CED Institute at UCCB has done so. Its aim is to ask people the right questions, rather than to offer them standard answers. Enabling, facilitating and animating, by a body such as the CED Institute, helps individuals, groups and communities to identify the origins of their problems, and assists them in deciding what to do tomorrow.

Community development has always been a fuzzy concept, and before people can act effectively, they must come to terms with the internal dynamics of communities (and their own being), and the nature of the world beyond their boundaries. The CED style should be friendly, responsive and open. To this end, the CED Institute examines demands made on it and classifies its response as follows:

(a) We can't help you with your problem, but we can identify someone who can;

(b) We can't help you with your problem on our own, but we can set up a joint venture with you, or with another learning organization to work on it;

(c) We **can** help you with your problem through the resources we have in teaching, research and publication. (This enabling function feeds back to the three traditional roles of the university in Canada.)

Universities can offer a space and place where people with diverse and different interests come together to discuss ways of launching ventures to serve their communities. As repositories of historical material, they can uncover lessons from the past to guide us to the future. They can provide a context for social action that avoids the excesses of individualism on the one hand and blind collectivism on the other. Because of their presence and prestige in society, universities can offer continuity for local efforts at human improvement. Most of all, they can inculcate some sense of spirituality, values and ethics into debate and action to create better worlds and handle the pressing problems of our time. And they can begin to respect local learning and knowledge which tends to get lost in the academic world because it does not fit into traditional intellectual frameworks.

Universities can offer continuity and stability in a community. They can offer a fixed point of reference for anyone interested in learning about CED. The CED Institute at UCCB serves as the quiet centre on the campus for those interested in CED. It is a place to which people outside the University can come to determine who is doing what and to what effect in CED, in Cape Breton, Nova Scotia, Canada and the world. It is a place for discussion about how people at the local level can become empowered participants in their personal and community development.

Across Canada, people in marginal areas and depressed communities such as Cape Breton are refusing to be victims or bystanders in the projects and programmes launched to help them. Informing and involving people to take charge of their lives has worked in the past and is being carried out effectively now. There are no experts in CED, only "learners." Through collective, collegial and co-operative action, universities can share their knowledge so that community development can offer something of value to baffled and bewildered people seeking to create a better life for themselves, their children and their communities.

ENDNOTES

1. James A. Christenson and Jerry W. Robinson, Jr., *Community Development in America.* Ames, Iowa: The Iowa State University, 1980.

2. Both requirements of publishing and community service have made significant inroads into Canada's 20th-century academy. Once relegated a distant third to teaching and research, scholarly publishing is now a prerequisite, and "a crucial part of a university professor's role." Since simple research is "untested and untried, ...the purpose of publishing one's research results is to test one's conclusions and ideas against the judgement of one's peers." Service to the university and community, at one time a neglected criterion, has become increasing important in the contemporary university: "the university professor's contract states that his [her] duties are to be found in the areas of teaching, service to the university and community, and research and publication." See David J. Bercuson, Robert Bothwell, and J. L. Granatstein, *The Great Brain Robbery: Canada's Universities on the Road to Ruin.* Toronto: McClelland and Stewart, 1984, pp. 108-11.

3. Jim Lotz, "The Beginning of Community Development in English Speaking Canada," in *Community Organizing: Canadian Experiences*, Brian Wharf and Michael Clague, eds. Oxford University Press, Toronto, 1997, pp. 22-23.

4. A. Davies, "A Prairie Dust Devil: The Rise and Decline of a Research Institute," in *Human Organization* 27(1), 1968, pp. 56-63.

5. Ibid.

6. Department of Agriculture and Immigration, Government of Manitoba, *A Study of the Population of Indian Ancestry Living in Manitoba.* Government of Manitoba: Winnipeg, 1959, p. 109.

7. Jean Lagassé, "Community Development in Manitoba," in *Human Organization*, 20(4) (Winter 1961-62): pp. 234.

8. Michael Schratz and Rob Walker, *Research as Social Change: New Opportunities for Qualitative Research.* London and New York, Routledge, 1995.

9. General Sir George Ainslie, quoted in Lotz, Pat and Jim, *Cape Breton Island.* Vancouver: Douglas, David and Charles, 1974, p. 50.

10. For more information on this remarkable man, see Jim Lotz and Michael Welton, *Father Jimmy: The Life and Times of Father Jimmy Tompkins.* Wreck Cove, Cape Breton: Breton Books, 1997

11. In 1939 Father Coady's book, *Masters of Their Own Destiny,* New York: Harper and Row, appeared, summarizing the achievements of the Movement he led.

12. Silver Donald Cameron, "Whither UCCB? A Certain Degree of Difference," in *New Maritimes*, November/December, 1995, p. 5.

13. Ibid. p. 6.

14. Ibid.

15. Peter Berger and Richard Neuhaus, *To Empower People: The Role of Mediating Structures in Public Policy.* Washington: American Enterprise Institute for Public Policy Research, 1977.

16. Gertrude MacIntyre, *Active Partners: Education and Local Development.* Sydney: UCCB Press, 1995.

2

THE COMMUNITY BUSINESS CORPORATION: *LA EMPRESA SOCIAL*
GREG MACLEOD

The year 1996 was a turning point in public attitude towards large business corporations. In the developed world, corporations were reporting huge profits, yet at the same time, they were carrying out radical downsizing. Even people who are normally conservative and uncritical found this difficult to understand and justify. If a business lost money, layoffs could be understood easily. But when a company made money and laid off those who helped make the money, then this was difficult to digest.

In the 1960s, antipoverty activists, students and labour leaders led in the anti-Establishment struggle. Today, Establishment leaders are themselves raising fundamental questions. In the February 1997 issue of *Atlantic Monthly*, George Soros claimed that the main threat to social justice and economic stability now comes from the uninhibited pursuit of laissez-faire economics. Soros says that the current free market system is a totalitarian system that will destroy the open society to which most Western intellectuals aspire. This position would not be surprising if it came from a left-wing ideologue. However, billionaire George Soros is one of the world's most successful capitalists. Still he points out that the dogma of equilibrium between supply and demand as a control system simply does not work in the world of international finance. He should know: he made his fortune through international financial trading.

Robert Reich, Secretary of Labor of the United States, aims his criticism at today's large, national and international business corporations. He has pointed out, in articles and in media interviews, that the modern business corporation is not serving society as it should. He finds it disturbing that so many business corporations are downsizing even as they are increasing profits. The reality is that government acts to improve the business climate and to improve technology, thus making it easier for large businesses to expand. This helps big businesses, but it does not help ordinary citizens. Government stimulation causes what is called a jobless recovery. Reich says that we may have to design a new kind of business corporation. This paper proposes that a new form is, in fact, evolving.

New forms are slowly emerging as the result of years of social activism by many organizers of community development. As a writer, my critique is not simply the result of intellectual inquiry. It is the result of lived experience and activist experimentation. My distrust of conventional, large business corporations goes back to my youth in Sydney Mines, Nova Scotia. As a schoolboy in the 1950s, I became involved in a form of community economic development. I had a savings account at the British Canadian Co-operative, a local credit union and co-operative. I still remember our family membership number, 255. In high school, I also joined the Princess Credit Union, named after our ancient coal mine.

It is difficult to grow up in a coal-mining community and not be aware of social injustice. Being brought up as one of nine children of a widow, I had a very distinct perspective on the world, especially when trying to get credit became a game of chance. When children were sent off to shop for everyday necessities, and when their families' debt had gone beyond the limit at the co-op, they had to test the other stores for credit. Money came from the coal mine, and the people in charge were unknown. Yet they had great power over who got a job and how much they got paid. From such experiences, I learned that power, wealth and control was always in some far distant place. Things were always controlled by the people from "away," who had no interest whatsoever in the well-being of the local people.

When I went to Xavier College in Sydney to begin my undergraduate studies, I got involved as a student worker, driving foreign visitors around to look at our co-ops and credit unions. Those visitors were looking for solutions to their problems of poverty and unemployment. Later, at St. Francis Xavier University in Antigonish, in spite of the pioneer work of its Extension Department, the only contact students had with issues of social justice came through one priest teaching sociology there, Reverend John Angus Rankin. The rest of the faculty seemed to think that local social-economic reform was not academically relevant. After theological studies in the seminary, I was sent to work with an old parish priest, Reverend Michael Gillis, who had been part of the St. F.X. Extension movement in the old days. He insisted that I read both left-wing and right-wing literature, and encouraged me to think independently. He disagreed with the evolution of St. Francis Xavier University, and he taught me to beware of institutions and to avoid "isms," such as communism or capitalism. He had served in World War II and knew what was going on in Europe. His experience of war helped dissipate any confidence he had had in ideologies.

His notion of religion was broad and liberal. For instance, he considered that money was a tool that could be used for good or bad. He always regretted having to put the weekly parish collection into the bank, but at that time there was nowhere else to put it. He longed for institutions guided by principles of social responsibility. By turning money over to selfish financiers, we gave them a powerful tool to oppress the poor. Or so he thought.

Gillis taught that helping people to live fuller lives was part of the religious mission. He told me that my job was to go out and help those in need. When I asked what needs I should address, he said, "You're a big boy now, with lots of education. You should be able to figure that out yourself." Armed with this advice, I proceeded to work immediately in organizing an association in one of the poor parts of town and helped unemployed residents get a hearing at Town Council. This kind of practical experience provided me with a great deal of material for reflection later on.

It was only in the late 1960s, while studying at Louvain in Belgium, that I became involved in critical discussion of social justice. During this period, Europe was alive with student movements for social reform. When I went to Oxford for postgraduate studies in Philosophy, I gained my credentials as an activist by going to jail. A social justice group to which I belonged discovered a blatant case of racial discrimination in the heart of Oxford: a hair stylist refused to accept black clients. We students arranged a sit-in on the sidewalk in front of the shop and were soon carried off to jail. We had agreed that our resistance would be passive, so that the "bobbies" had to carry us away as we sang "We Shall Overcome." We were ushered into jail politely by the bobbies and kept there for the day.

We were eventually tried and fined for disturbing the peace. It soon became apparent to me that this type of activism was somewhat of a charade that did not accomplish a great deal. It simply made middle-class people feel that they were on the side of the angels. That same year, I went to Poland and Czechoslovakia to look at the co-operative movement. In Prague, I was impressed by a progressive parliamentarian who wished to preserve socialist morality but who saw the necessity of changing the methods of seeking it.

He saw clearly how free-market pricing could be a means of improving the efficiency of production. Listening to him complain about the Russian inability to distinguish between ends and means helped me understand the economic failure of the co-operatives at home. On reflection, I began to see that our co-operative activists were wonderful as far as moral intentions were concerned—but terrible at the level of means.

Along with so many others, I was inspired by the ideals and personal commitment of the sixties. In retrospect, we see that they laid the groundwork for long term attitudinal changes, but the ideals were not translated into new social economic structures for most people. My own background inclined me to look at the economic implications for the ordinary citizen and to resist movements involving only "enlightened" enthusiasts. To me, so many of those groups came to resemble secular monasteries, espousing ideals which, though admirable were beyond the reach of most people. I have always preferred to promote changes related to the formation of new economic structures which can survive in the world of the average citizen.

After five years of study in Europe, I travelled for a few months in Latin America and there I saw firsthand the face of poverty and injustice. Coming home through Toronto and Halifax, I was struck by the difference between the wealthy developed world and the poverty of the Third World. However, when I finally reached Cape Breton Island, I had the distinct impression that I was back in the Third World. Poverty and unemployment were rampant: governments and large corporations were concentrated in the centres of wealth and influence.

When I began to teach at the University College of Cape Breton, I remembered Dr. Jimmy Tompkins, a pioneer in the old St. F.X. Extension movement, who claimed that university professors had a moral obligation to use their knowledge and technology for the betterment of the community.[1]

Tompkins was the founder of the first credit union in English speaking Canada and of the first co-operative housing project in North America.[2] His example inspired me to orient the Tompkins Institute at UCCB to an analysis of unemployment in the local community. I was disappointed in the economic achievements of the co-operatives set up by Tompkins and his Extension Department colleagues in the 1930s. The older British Canadian Co-operative system, set up in 1900, had grown and prospered to sales of over $50 million in 1950. In contrast, the assets of the Extension Department's co-operatives were well under that level even by the 1970s. The British Canadian Co-operative went bankrupt in the late 1970s, and the Extension co-operatives grew hardly at all. Struck by the poor record of co-operatives in Nova Scotia and the rapid growth of conventional business corporations, I decided to make the business co-operative a research theme, using a methodology of action-research.

While small business is becoming more important in the modern economy, there is still no doubt that the main actors in the economy, the ones determining the shape of our society, are large business corporations. So if we wish to change the social economic system, we have to change the business corporation. There is a developing consensus that a middle form must be developed, neither government agency, nor traditional private business, a form sometimes referred to as the "third sector." However, this sector includes more than business: it includes the broad range of voluntary organizations referred to by Dr. Jack Quarter of the University of Toronto.[3] In this chapter, I claim that new forms are, in fact, emerging. It is true that some conventional shareholder corporations, like "The Body Shop" and "Ben and Jerry's," are becoming philanthropic. Such corporations have adopted special ethics such as environmentalism and donation to charities. However, this is not a basic shift in control and structure. In this chapter, I claim that fundamental new forms, such as the "community business corporation," are evolving. I will discuss that terminology and then present a composite view.

THE CORPORATION

Historically, the term "corporation" is much broader than the reduced version we have today. Monks in a monastery, members of a medieval stonemasons' guild or the professors at Oxford University were all regarded as a corporation. They acted as one body or *corpus* to carry out a mission assigned to them by a higher authority outside of the corporation. The authority could be political or religious. Once the medieval *corpus* was formed, it was understood that it could be directed to a variety of goals. (Sometimes, it is difficult for the modern student to understand that a body of individuals can act as one collectivity, given the force of individualism and self-interest that dominates our world.)

In Renaissance times, the corporation became secularized. In the new age of individual rights, the value of the collective community became weaker. Gradually, the concept of the corporation became perverted by the laissez-faire capitalists of the 19th century. The University of Chicago economist, Milton Friedman, claims that self-interest is necessary for growth. For him, corporations must become institutionalized and legitimized greed seekers: "The only obligation which business has in and to society is to get on with the job of producing profit for its shareholders...the managers are the agents appointed to carry out the purpose of the shareholders."[4]

Kenneth Goodpaster of Harvard University disagrees with this mechanistic view of corporations:

> "We think an analogy holds between the individual and the corporation. If we analyze the concept of moral responsibility as it applies to persons, we find that projecting it to corporations as agents in society is possible."[5]

L.C.B. Gower, a prominent authority on the history of law, also disagrees with Friedman. In his standard textbook,[6] Gower writes that modern corporations have little relationship to the legal intent with which they were established by lawmakers in the United Kingdom and North America. Gower points out that shareholder ownership of business corporations is a legal fiction. Rather, they are merely lenders of capital; the real controllers are the managing directors. He suggests that it is time to reform the corporation and submit it to a more appropriate guidance. The corporation is a legal person; as such, it seems reasonable that we speak of it as having responsibilities and purposes other than simple profit-making. In British and Canadian law, corporations must still present a Memorandum of Association which outlines their purposes. However, Gower is optimistic in assuring us that the law will eventually catch up. For him, as for Robert Reich, corporations are creatures of law, and while the law always lags behind reality, it will eventually be reformed to reflect reality.

By now, it is clear that the corporation was not invented by Henry Ford. Besides university and monastic corporations, we have had business corporations for hundreds of years. The two oldest corporations in the world happen to have branches in Cape Breton: Stora from Sweden, incorporated in the 14th century, and the original British Hudson's Bay Company, incorporated in 1670.

While I recognize that the corporate form is used in many sectors, such as hospitals and universities, I wish to deal here only with business corporations. Classically, the corporation is an entity on its own; it is a combination of capital and human resources organized so as to achieve goals laid down by a board of directors through efficient management of economic wealth. The ownership of the corporation is secondary and relative. The form of ownership can vary, but the production of goods and services in a collective manner is a constant element in the corporation.

The concept of ownership of corporations has varied over the years. When Hudson's Bay was incorporated in 1670, a group of individuals owned shares, but fundamentally the corporation was an agent of the Crown. In 1780, the Lord Admiral of the Fleet asked the Company to carry out explorations in the North of Canada. The corporation refused, since all its vessels were tied up in the fur trade. In retaliation, the Lord Admiral threatened to have the king abrogate the privileges of the corporation and to dissolve it. For the Admiral, the very existence of a royally incorporated corporation depended on service to the realm.[7]

In the history of the Western World, large business corporations have done a lot of harm but they have also done a lot of good. They constitute a powerful instrument for economic change. It is a serious mistake for those involved in social reform to discount the utility of corporate techniques. In calling for a return to free enterprise small business controlled by individual entrepreneurs, people forget that we are able to enjoy automobiles and airplanes only because the corporate form allowed groups of individuals to work together in one structure to achieve what they, as individuals, could not. During the last few hundred years, it has become apparent that the modern corporation as a form of business has been the engine of development for the modern economy.

Today, the legal ownership of corporations is structured in different ways:

1. Some are owned by shareholders through the purchase of shares. Often owners are distant, as is the case in most large corporations, such as Ford and Lockheed.

2. Other corporations are owned co-operatively by their employees or customers.

3. Others are not-for-profit, effectively owned by the community at large. These I call community business corporations (CBCs).

Whether a corporation is owned by a co-operative group, a local community, or by distant shareholders, it is still an entity producing goods or services through the manipulation of capital resources. The corporate entity can be managed well or poorly, whatever its ownership. It can be directed to improvement of the community, or to enrichment of the private owners. Sometimes, the two motives coincide in their effect; at other times, they do not. Especially in developing countries and in poorer parts of developed countries, large, non-resident corporations have depleted the local community. Regardless of how efficiently the corporation produces, the critical element is its purpose or goal. This brings us back to the basic question, "Does it exist for the sake of the shareholders, or for the sake of the community?" A corporation's shareholders may be capitalist or co-operative. Some co-operatives explicitly take on a broad community purpose; others do not. It seems almost self-evident that a corporation owned by a local community group would be more inclined to seek the good of the local community, at least as part of its goal.

Community Business Corporations

The gravest threats to community come from non-resident ownership of economic resources. Hence for us, the community, a specific geographic place, becomes the essential agent of change. As the word suggests, community refers to what we have and share in common. Sharing a piece of land is not sufficient to make a community. The community is determined intentionally.

The very word "business" frequently raises hackles

amongst socially progressive, community-minded people: they blame business for much of what is wrong in the world and equate business with greed and selfishness. I would define business as the production of goods and services to be exchanged for other goods and services produced by society. Money is a medium of exchange that makes the exchange more efficient. Upon reflection, we can see how harm can be done when community activists oppose business indiscriminately. I understand the term business in a very common sense manner, and I consider that it represents an honourable and necessary social activity. Business and greed can be divorced. Business can serve community.

In the United States, the term "community development corporation" is frequently used to describe the type of business we are talking about. I prefer not to use this term. Its connotation has become too broad to be useful. CDCs carry on a broad range of activities: they build schools and houses, they help minority businesses, and they perform many other useful societal activities. Usually, they are seen as an instrument to help minority and marginalized groups to participate in mainstream society.

In Canada, the community business movement is more likely to have arisen out of the co-operative movement. It is more likely to be an attempt to reform the social-economic system in general, rather than simply to integrate minority groups into the general society. Not surprisingly, it is the most active in areas of high unemployment, usually geographically marginalized areas, with pressing need for infrastructure and enabling agents of development. I will discuss a couple of community business corporations and then, I will go on to discuss the CBC model.

New Dawn Enterprises is one of the oldest community business corporations in Canada. New Dawn Enterprises was established in Cape Breton in 1974 by a group of professors from the University College of Cape Breton together with other local citizens concerned about economic decline. New Dawn's structure is a not-for-profit mother corporation having a number of subsidiaries. It responds to the expressed needs of the community. Over the past two decades, New Dawn has established a large real-estate portfolio: affordable housing for people on low and medium income, a home for the aged, dental centres, home nursing, a volunteer resource centre, and a wide variety of job-creation schemes. With 100 employees and a yearly payroll of almost $2 million, New Dawn is self-sustaining, able to generate sufficient revenue to cover expenses and fund new developments. In 1997, its assets were $20 million, mainly in real estate. It is considered a private sector body with a business structure flexible enough to enable it to respond to a variety of community needs.

A more recent community business corporation is Cape Breton's BCA Holdings, a community finance corporation with more than a million dollars in assets. BCA raises investment money, pays a return, and invests in local job-creating businesses. BCA has reconstituted a number of bankrupt companies, such as a high-tech rope company and a radio station. It owns a small hotel. While BCA received an interest-free loan from a federal agency, neither it nor New Dawn has received government grants to this date.

BCA is a particularly important experiment because it deals in finance. At the end of the 20th century, financial institutions have become an extremely important force in determining the course of humanity. Movements of capital have become international in the new global economy. National governments have very little control over the decisions of the international financial system. A few large financial players can change the financial markets with a few strategic decisions; this can affect interest rates and the relative values of national currencies. The decisions of large corporations can affect government bond-ratings and trigger programmes of national austerity and cutbacks. Thus decisions in Tokyo or Hong Kong can determine whether a small business in Toronto, northern Manitoba or Cape Breton will survive. The idea behind BCA is that a local finance corporation can help make a local community more self-sufficient. Local capital and local investment help insulate the community from outside forces.

In Spain, the best examples of alternative corporate forms are in Mondragon and Valencia, both of them variations on the co-operative system. Begun in 1952, the Mondragon complex numbers approximately 100 worker-owned enterprises, as well as a university, a bank and various research centres. With over 30,000 worker-owners producing a wide variety of products, from dishwashers to forklifts to automobile parts, it is one of the most commercially successful alternative business corporations in the world. In 1997, total assets amounted to more than $13 billion; annual sales exceeded $6 billion. All of the parts of the Mondragon enterprise are integrated through interlocking boards of directors and common commercial strategies. They now call their complex a "co-operative corporation." It is worth noting that while so many large business corporations were downsizing in 1996, Mondragon initiated an expansion plan to create 8,000 new jobs in four years. In Valencia, a group of social reformers, inspired by the Mondragon example, began in the early 1970s to develop a similar system of community owned businesses: a bank, a retail chain, a college and a number of factories, all united under one umbrella organization.

In Italy, the Emilia-Romagna area has generated still another form of corporate business, using a strategy of clustering co-operatives and small private businesses into strategic combinations. Most of these businesses are community-owned, but they act as one unit through various joint ventures and marketing co-operatives. With a population of 3.9 million, Emilia-Romagna has 90,000 small manufacturing enterprises. All collaborate so that instead of competing with each other, they compete with other regions. The result is that the area's unemployment rate was a mere 4.7 percent in 1996.

All of the examples we have discussed are rooted in a specific geographic area. In all, community pride and commitment to neighbour translate into economic benefit. Their strategy is to use the local human and physical resources to increase local self-sufficiency and wellbeing.

A COMPOSITE CONCEPT

From my involvement in our own modest experience in Cape Breton and my observation of other experiences, I propose a new model of a community business corporation as an agent of change. In this century, the business corporation has become accepted as a conventional non-governmental instrument or agent for economic activity in most industrialized countries. Corporate enterprises such as General Motors, Fiat, Siemens, or Shell Oil are collections of capital, people, and technologies organized to produce goods and services and generate profit for shareholders.

For those involved in local economic development, conventional corporations present a major obstacle. They are usually controlled by absentee owner shareholders, and so have little commitment to the local community. Now more than ever, they are mobile, moving from country to country in response to economic enticement. In the name of efficiency and global competitiveness they shut down branch plants and move to other countries. Their actions have caused high unemployment in many poor and depleted communities. If we view the business corporation as a corporate person, we see that the key problem lies in overall intent. In a conventional corporation, the primary intent is to increase profits for the private use of shareholders. The welfare of the community where the corporation functions is secondary. In contrast, the rationale and intent of the Community Business Corporation is to promote and develop the local community.

In many countries, the traditional form of community economics has been the co-operative movement. However, the co-operative form has proved inadequate in the face of radical economic changes during the last 30 years or so. The co-operative sector has been concentrated in the retail-consumer area, and in domestic finance through credit unions. It has not been flexible enough to create jobs and ensure economic survival in marginal economies. Although the co-operative is a vast improvement over the traditional corporation, the primary intent or concern of co-operatives, in general, is the well-being of a special interest group: member-consumers or employees. Co-operatives normally claim to represent the good of their own members; usually, they do not aspire to meet broader community needs. It is, nonetheless, distinct in that its central intent is the well-being of the *overall community* where it carries out its business. Hence, job creation is usually a major objective of a community enterprise, like a co-operative, especially given contemporary high unemployment.

Traditional corporations, as well as today's mega-co-operatives, are often controlled by absentee managers. Moreover, in both, the assets are owned by individuals, not by the community. We need a new concept, a new understanding of what a corporate form can be. Perhaps this new structure should be considered a neoco-operative, since it is a reformulation of the co-operative ideal. Alex Laidlaw, a pioneer in the Canadian co-operative movement, was thinking along these lines when he said that co-operatives would have to reinvent themselves or become irrelevant to social economic reform. In 1975, at a meeting of community activists in Acadia University, Laidlaw said that:

> "If credit unions and co-operatives are not a
> distinctly different kind of business, if they are

not a reform movement, a social movement oriented to change, then perhaps the poor and those who are left outside the mainstream of our society will have to build a separate movement of their own, maybe with Community Development Corporations, to serve their needs and exert leverage on the power structures."[8]

At the International Co-operative Alliance in 1980, he presented the following recommendation:

"...the creation of clusters of specialized co-operatives or a single multipurpose society, especially in urban areas in such a way as to provide a wide range of economic and social services: housing, credit, banking, insurance, restaurants, industrial enterprises, medical services, tourism, recreation, etc. within the scope of a single neighbourhood co-operative complex."[9]

Within the community economic development movement as well as within the traditional co-operative movement, there seems to be consensus that we need new corporate institutions to function in a more socially responsible manner. In Britain, the term "community enterprise" is used for these new corporations. There, community enterprises have usually arisen to respond to high unemployment in areas such as Glasgow in Scotland. The idea always is that the corporation can become an enabling instrument for the local community to solve its own problems and control its own future. The Plunkett Foundation of Oxford outlined the characteristics of a community enterprise:[10]

1.   A community enterprise is a business which aims to create sustainable jobs and related

training opportunities for local people and/or to provide commercial services.

2. A community enterprise aims to make profits and to become financially self-supporting; to use profits only for investment in its enterprises, for limited bonus payments to workers, and for community benefit.

3. Membership or share-holding in the community enterprise is organized on democratic one-person-one-vote principles.

4. A community enterprise must be registered either as a company or as a co-operative society using a model or other legal structure which is recognized as acceptable.

5. The assets of the community enterprise are owned on behalf of the community and are held in trust by the directors such that the assets may not be disposed of to benefit financially individual members or directors.

6. The membership of the community enterprise must be open to all persons within its agreed area of benefit. In some circumstances a "community of interest" or a "community of need" can be established.

7. The community enterprise is committed to being a good employer regarding wage levels, terms and conditions, equal opportunities and employee participation.

8. The community enterprise is committed to evaluating and reporting annually on the effectiveness of its impact on the local community.

A development organization called Community Business Scotland has settled upon the following as a definition of community enterprise:

> A community business is a trading organization which is owned and controlled by the local community and which aims to create ultimately self-supporting and viable jobs for local people in its area of benefit, and to use profits made from its business activities either to create more employment or to provide local services, or to support local charitable works. A community business is likely to have a multi-purpose enterprise and it may be based on a geographical community or on a community of interest.[11]

The community enterprise may or may not involve worker ownership, but it must always involve majority *local ownership and control*. A community business corporation like BCA or Chac Lol[12] resembles a conventional business in most of its operations. For instance, it must generate enough money to pay expenses and deal with management and control problems. However, it is profoundly different in its essence. The motivation of a community enterprise is community improvement. Profit is a means not an end in itself. A community enterprise is not owned simply by shareholders or workers. Rather, it holds property and assets as a trust and in the interest of the local community. A community enterprise is localized and builds on the local community; it is, normally, not moveable and not subject to being bought out. And a community enterprise depends upon volunteers.

The community enterprise can work in any business context, not simply in depleted communities. Whether we are simply reviving an older form, as Gower seems to suggest, or whether we are inventing something new, it is clear that a new form is evolving that is different. For me, the essence of a corporation is association in a common task. The members of the corporation participate in the production of a product or service. The fact that I hold a share certificate (a mere piece of paper) does not in itself mean that I am involved in a common process in any real sense. Lawyers refer to such cases as "legal fiction." Ordinary shareholders in large corporations like Ford or Shell are not associates. They are simply lenders of money, as Gower explains. Shareholders in small businesses and co-operatives, on the other hand, usually do participate in enterprises, size being an important determining factor here.

Even in a corporation based on association in a common task, questions of control and the division of authority arise. If control does not reside in ownership of shares, then on what basis does a board of directors operate? One suggestion may be to do as universities and hospitals do where the board serves *pro bono publico* (for the public good). Internal corporate decision-making structures are secondary, and are related to circumstances and culture. For instance, one type of management structure would be appropriate for a corporation composed of graduate engineers, while another type would be appropriate for a factory where the majority of workers are barely literate. Although the internal structures of a community business corporation may vary, the essential purpose is always improvement of the local community, not enrichment of non-resident shareholders. The important thing is to explore new possibilities. The details of structure and operation require a much more extensive treatment since they are closely related to the culture and general context of the community where the corporation is located.

The Key Issue

The most important theoretical issue here is whether social improvement is an adequate driving force. Will it stimulate corporations to create prosperity and jobs? Many business textbooks assume that the only adequate motivator of business enterprise is private profit. The organizers of community business corporations disagree. They propose that business corporations can be efficient and entrepreneurial, even when community improvement is the prevailing motive. For them, profit is a means, not an end. Whether a "do-gooder" business corporation can be efficient and profitable is fiercely debated. The best way to decide this issue is through empirical demonstration. When someone says it can't be done, we say, "But have you tried it?" Mondragon in Spain, Emilia-Romagna in Italy, New Dawn, BCA and others in Canada furnish abundant empirical proof that a community-oriented corporation can indeed operate efficiently and profitably in the modern global economy. What they constitute is an international movement, closely allied to the co-operative movement, which aims to bring about social economic reform. These enterprises differ in structure and in products and services rendered, but they share a basic set of communitarian values.

If we agree that a social collectivity such as the business corporation is defined by its purpose, then a shift in purpose necessarily means redefining the business corporation. If the purpose shifts from shareholder enrichment to an increase of jobs in the local community, the result is a community business corporation where the board of directors does not represent individual shareholders, who want higher dividends. Rather, the board represents the general local community, which desires development and improvement.

In the non-indigenous world of North America, the notion of relinquishing private ownership of property is a hard sell. Yet we know the answer to questions like "Does the sun or the moon or the air belong to anyone?" Environmental problems have made us admit that we do not own the air, that we are simply stewards of it. And we know that today's sophisticated commercial products, especially technological products, are really a patrimony, the product of many generations' efforts.

Indeed the most valuable part of the modern economy is knowledge, and knowledge isn't the private property of any one individual. While individuals do invent new things, their innovations always build on old knowledge. Perhaps now is the time to restore the classical notion of stewardship. Individuals must be responsible for specific economic goods, but theirs is never absolute control. Ownership must be subject to the demands of the larger common good. And some wealthy individuals, like George Soros, regard their role as one of stewardship, rather than absolute power over wealth gained through intelligent gambling on the stock market.

But Soros' stewardship, though admirable, is voluntary and isolated. Our proposal is to institutionalize stewardship in community business corporations. The business corporation is a proven vehicle for guaranteeing stable, long-term commitment to the community good. The pressing need for this new form of business corporation is evident in marginal communities. Conventional corporations abandon them and relocate in centres of wealth and power, removing, as they do, innovation. Firms left behind are usually less technologically and organizationally innovative, hence, less competitive. This is why the Italian and Spanish models are so interesting. They are communitarian, but they recognize their need for modern techniques if they are to survive. An innovative community needs local support for innovation, investment, technology upgrading, planning, training, and market development, all of which are necessary to ensure economic and cultural survival in marginal environments.[13] So for community groups to establish successful businesses, more than good will is required. They must find sources of technology and expertise. An obvious source is the local university or college, which includes a broad cross-section of experts. The experience of New Dawn, BCA and Mondragon are good illustrations of the local university providing technology transfer. In these cases, the community's university was the source of technical expertise.

When the Berlin Wall came down, it took with it the communist state economy of Eastern Europe. Many observers saw that devolution as proof that free-market capitalism was the only viable economic structure. Experience in the Western World, and in the former Soviet Bloc, now shows that neither state enterprise nor unbridled corporate enterprise is best. We live now in a time of experimentation, when we can and must try new hybrid structures. In our experimenting, we must insist that the economy is *for* people and the people are *not for* the economy. We no longer accept the blind necessities of Darwin, Smith or Marx. Most of us believe that we have choices and options in how we do business. Our belief is that a new, person-oriented economy will eventually dominate. If it does not, we may, as George Soros claims, destroy ourselves.

ENDNOTES
1. Rev. Dr. James Tompkins, *Knowledge for the People: A Call to St. Francis Xavier's College*. Antigonish: St. F.X. University, 1921.
2. Greg MacLeod, "Atlantic Canadian Roots," Ch.2 in *Community Economic Development in Canada*. David Douglas, Ed., Toronto: McGraw-Hill, 1995.
3. Jack Quarter, *Canada's Social Economy*. Toronto: James Lorimer, 1992.
4. Milton Friedman, *Free to Choose*. New York: Harcourt Brace, 1980, p. 50.
5. Kenneth Goodpaster, "Can a Corporation Have a Conscience?" in *Harvard Business Review*, Jan-Feb, 1982, p. 133.
6. L.C.B. Gower, *The Principles of Modern Company Law*. London: Stevens and Sons, 1969.

7. cf. Peter C. Newman, *Company of Adventurers*. Markham, Ontario: Viking/Penguin Books, 1985.

8. Alexander Laidlaw, "Outline of an Address," presented to a Community Development Workshop for the Atlantic Provinces, Wolfville, N.S., January 29, 1975, p. 12.

9. cf. Alexander Laidlaw, *The Atlantic Co-operator*, December 1980, p. 25.

10. Plunkett Foundation, *Yearbook of Co-operative Enterprise*. Oxford, UK, 1992, p. 30.

11. Calouste Gulbenkian Foundation, p. 4, *Community Business Works*, a report by the UK Branch, London, 1982.

12. Greg MacLeod, *From Mondragon to America: Experiments in Community Economic Development*. Sydney: UCCB Press, 1997, see chapter 7.

13. Charles Davis, "Innovation Support Services for Innovative Communities," pp. 71-94 in D. Bruce and M. Whitlaw, eds., *Community-Based Approaches to Rural Development*. Sackville, New Brunswick: Mount Allison University, 1993b.

3

STRUCTURAL CONSIDERATIONS IN THE CREATION OF A NOT-FOR-PROFIT CORPORATION
GARY CORSANO

Great attention has been focused on the reform of company legislation in Canada in the last 25 years. With a few exceptions, however, the reformation has been exclusively in the area of conventional companies limited by shares—for-profit corporations. The not-for-profit corporation has been ignored to the extent that even the Queen's Printer in Ottawa entirely omitted the Federal "not-for-profit" legislation from the most recent edition of the Revised Statutes of Canada. The downsizing of the public sector creates the need for non-governmental agencies to assume responsibility for services previously provided by government. This activity will cause bureaucrats, lawyers and legislators to focus greater attention on the role, structure and responsibilities of not-for-profit corporations.

Those who specialize in the area of corporate law for not-for-profit organizations, especially for community development corporations, must contend with the existing legislation. They hope that a clearly delineated legal structure will give greater definition, purpose and direction to community-building through these particular forms of business associations.

To the uninitiated, the notion of a community development corporation (CDC) conjures up the image of an organization in which the roles of the participants are well-defined and the idea of the community, to whom the organization is accountable, is clear. Until recently, however, that type of clarity—of the sort that a lawyer, from a legal point of view, or a banker, from a financial perspective, is obsessed with—has not been present.

Where sophisticated individuals in the private sector would spend considerable time defining their relationship to one another before embarking on a business enterprise, the individuals in a not-for-profit community development corporation may focus on the project at hand: the business plan, financial projections, and so forth.

There are explanations for this lack of clarity. Not-for-profit, community-based business enterprises are a relatively recent phenomenon. The legislative framework for them is not readily apparent, and the financial costs associated with hiring lawyers to establish and maintain a legal framework may be thought unnecessary.

To focus energy on legal details amidst the crises in which CDC proponents find their communities may seen like "fiddling while Rome burns." Leaders in the CDC movement tend to come from fields other than business and law. They tend to see the "corporation" not as the miracle child of 19th and 20th century commerce, but as an agent of destructive liberal capitalism.

Concern about internal legal structures will expand as CDCs play a greater role in communities, interacting increasingly with private, public and third-sector organizations. This is not to suggest, however, that one type of corporate structure should apply universally. Economic, educational and cultural circumstances will dictate structure. Whatever structure is established, the community should understand it. This is particularly important since government is placing greater personal obligations on directors of for-and not-for-profit businesses for statutory matters like payment of source deductions, provincial sales tax, goods and services tax and compliance with environmental legislation and regulations.

This chapter is not a manual for incorporating a not-for-profit corporation. This is a task better left to the experts in each of the jurisdictions throughout the country. Instead, this chapter comments on some salient features of the not-for-profit corporation and compares it with the for-profit corporation. Further, it compares types of not-for-profit corporations, examining the issue of appropriate incorporating legislation and, most importantly, exploring the notion of governance and accountability in the not-for-profit corporation.

Not-for-profit corporations share many characteristics with for-profit corporations. Each is a creature of statute that comes into existence following a particular piece of legislation (in some cases the same legislation) and by the registration and issuance of certain documents by a government official of the incorporating jurisdiction.

Both have by-laws or articles of association which, subject to the incorporating legislation, govern the manner in which each organization is run. The by-laws or articles of association establish the manner in which an individual acquires membership in the corporation, how its Board of Directors and officers are selected, and the way in which corporate business is conducted through meetings of the members or directors. What distinguishes the not for-profit corporation from its for-profit counterpart is the fundamental purpose of each. In simplest terms, the for-profit corporation's purpose is to return a profit to its members (more commonly referred to as shareholders).

In contrast, the not-for-profit corporation is defined in

terms of its objects or purposes, as set out in the corporation's constituting documents, sometimes called the memorandum of association, articles of association or charter. Returning a profit to individual members is prohibited. According to Gower, companies which are formed for a purpose other than the profit of their members are "merely a more modern and convenient substitute for the trust."[1]

As in any other corporation, the liability of the members of a not-for-profit corporation is limited, subject, as mentioned earlier, to statutory provisions which impose obligations on the directors of both for-profit and not-for-profit corporations.

No member in his or her individual capacity is liable for any debt or liability of the not-for-profit corporation beyond the amount which the by-laws or the articles of association of the corporation prescribe. Usually this amount is nominal. For this reason, not-for-profit corporations are referred to as "limited corporations," and the words "society," "association," "limited," "incorporated," "corporation," or an abbreviation thereof form a part of the not-for-profit corporation's name. Not-for-profit corporations fall into two general categories: those formed for social or charitable purposes (usually referred to as societies or associations), and those formed to carry out a trade, industry or business, usually for the benefit of a particular community (however broadly or narrowly the word "community" may be construed). Organizations such as the Cancer Society, church altar guilds and local bird-watching clubs are examples of the former; New Dawn Enterprises Limited, BCA Holdings Limited, and other community development corporations illustrate the latter.

For the purposes of the *Income Tax Act (Canada)*, both types of not-for-profit corporations are treated in the same manner, in that no member of either type can obtain any pecuniary gain from the corporation. Nor may the not-for-profit corporation build up excessive reserves or retained earnings.

Instead, there is an obligation to ensure that these funds are spent in accordance with the corporation's objects.

The distinction between the two types of not-for-profit corporations is important to the scope of corporate power and authority which the incorporating legislation permits.

Some individuals have wrongfully assumed that because the corporation they wish to create is a "not-for-profit" corporation, any incorporating statute will do to incorporate them. They fail to recognize that the legislation through which the corporation gains its existence may limit the types of activities which the corporation can carry out.

To put it another way, the corporation they create may not have the legal capacity to do certain things. For example, in Nova Scotia, sub-section 3(1) of the *Societies Act* specifies that:

> ...a society may be incorporated under this act to promote any benevolent, philanthropic, patriotic, religious, charitable, artistic, literary, educational, social, professional, recreational or sporting or any other useful object, but not for the purpose of carrying on any trade, industry or business.[2]

Subsection 3(1) significantly limits the types of activities in which a corporation incorporated under this legislation can partake. It could not, for example, run or participate in running a store, hotel, manufacturing facility, commercial leasing business, or a commercial radio station. These activities would be clearly *ultra vires* the company, and would undermine the principle of limited liability. Thus they would expose the members to personal liability for matters arising out of those activities, because the advantages go beyond the not-for-profit corporation's legal capacity.

If the incorporating legislation prohibited a not-for-profit corporation from carrying on business, and if, after entering into a contractual obligation, the not-for-profit corporation was unable to meet its obligations under the contract, the aggrieved party could commence an action against the members of the not-for-profit corporation in their personal capacity. It could argue that because the not-for-profit corporation could not itself legally enter into the contract, the legally contracting party can only be its individual members. If serious consideration is not given at the outset to the range of activities in which the proposed not-for-profit corporation will be engaged, the consequences for its members or directors may be significant.

If the individuals incorporating the not-for-profit corporation are uncertain as to the range of activities in which their corporation may become engaged, it would be beneficial for them to incorporate under corporate legislation. This would allow the adoption of the broadest objects and powers, thereby allowing greater flexibility as circumstances change over time.

In either type of not-for-profit corporation, issues of governance and accountability arise. However, these issues are more complicated in theory and in practice for CDCs than for not-for-profit corporations that have specific social or charitable purposes. The latter's objects and purposes are generally narrow, and the constituency, to whom the directors are accountable, can be clearly identified. Such is not the case with CDCs.

For example, the directors of the Cancer Society would have a fairly clear mandate to spend money raised by the organization on cancer research. They would not be at liberty, however, to contribute to arthritis research. The executive of the church altar guild would have to use its funds to purchase linens, vestments, candles or related articles. The local birdwatching club would have to use its funds for educational ornithological pursuits; it could not finance a member's fledgling binocular franchise.

Similarly, in a conventional corporation limited by shares, the directors are required, by the members or shareholders, to account for their actions regularly. Issues ranging from failure to return a profit to shareholders, to the violation of fiduciary duties, may result in the removal of directors.

In each of these examples, the directors (the individuals entrusted with the authority to make decisions on behalf of the organization) are called upon to account for their actions by the organization's members—some of whom may be the same people who entrusted the directors in the first place. This is fairly straightforward.

A particular problem arises, however, with governance and accountability in CDCs since they fashion themselves as organizations impressed with a trust for the benefit of the entire community in which they carry on business. To draw on the language of the law of trusts, the settlor of the trust is the community, the trustee is the community, and the beneficiary is the community. As Professor Greg MacLeod put it: "A community enterprise is not owned by shareholders or workers but operates as a trust in the interest of the local community."[3]

Ownership, albeit in trust, rests in the community. Accordingly, it follows that the community has ultimate control over the organization. If this were taken to its extreme, it could be argued that each citizen in the community in which the CDC exists would somehow have a "democratic" right to take part in the CDCs decision-making process, in the election of directors, appointment of officers, approval of budgets, appointment of auditors, and a host of other matters. Indeed, it is conceivable that every citizen would have a right to vote on every issue.

There are some who champion this type of participatory democracy in community economic development. There are those who would even suggest that failure to allow such participation undermines the very notion of community economic development, and further, that CDCs cannot rightly use the word "community" without being truly democratic.

While CDCs must give concrete meaning to the notion of "community" in matters of governance and accountability, attributing democratic rights to citizens in the community in which the CDC exists would not help to create or maintain a strong business enterprise. On the contrary, to thus extend the democratic principle may undermine the enterprise's ability to serve the community.

Such volatility may make third parties less apt to enter into long-term arrangements with CDCs. For example, lending institutions do not wish to lend money to a business in which the players could suddenly and radically change because of a possible take-over by another group. Operating a business is difficult enough when one person has control. Adding contingencies such as a significant shift or change in leadership only makes the task more onerous. It is also less likely that another individual or group would wish to enter into a joint venture with an organization so broadly based.

This is not to suggest, however, that the notion of community should be so amorphous or intangible that the directors are never accountable to any real citizens in the community in which the CDC carries on business. Structures must be created to enhance and give true meaning to the notion of community, while maintaining the continuity essential in sustaining a business enterprise.

Within the corporate structure of New Dawn Enterprises Limited and its associated companies, the sense of community and continuity has been achieved by having the existing members select, from the community, a cross-section of individuals from various backgrounds. Thus business people, trade unionists, outreach and community workers, educators and academics all become members of the company. From that group, a smaller sub-group is elected to the board of directors. Term limits, both for general and for Board of Directors, ensure that new blood is regularly injected into the organization. The induction of new individuals, however, is gradual, thereby ensuring continuity. Members of the company (the representative group of the community) have the right to exercise ultimate control at any time, and an annual meeting of members provides opportunity to question the Board of Directors.

The New Dawn model may not be the best corporate structure for all CDCs. It was created to meet the needs of an expanding organization, one which required a regime to allow for orderly change over time. Changing circumstances may result in a change in its structure.

What is universal in the corporate structures of CDCs is their need to enliven the notion of community, to give it real meaning. The CDC that does not do so may be seen to be a "closed shop." If that happens, the CDCs contributions to the economic life of the community are little different than those of other business. It is not, then, truly a "community" development corporation.

ENDNOTES
1. L.C.B. Gower, *The Principles of Modern Company Law.* London: Stevens and Sons, 1969.
2. *Nova Scotia Societies Act*, Sub-Section 3(1).
3. Greg MacLeod, *New Age Business: Community Corporations That Work.* Ottawa: Canada Council on Social Development, 1986.

PART 2

EMPIRICAL CASES IN COMMUNITY ECONOMIC DEVELOPMENT

4

NEW DAWN ENTERPRISES LIMITED: A COMMUNITY ECONOMIC DEVELOPMENT EXPERIMENT
RANKIN MACSWEEN

The purpose of this chapter is to provide an overview of New Dawn Enterprises Ltd. It consists of a brief description of New Dawn's beginning, a summary of its present activities and an analysis of the organization from several perspectives. New Dawn's history parallels the history of Cape Breton Island, particularly the Island's patterns of underdevelopment; it evokes the culture of Cape Breton, highlighting those features that prejudice the Island's economic circumstances. These things inform New Dawn's organizational structure, and distinguish differences from the conceptual elements and developmental processes which that organization shares with the community development movement in North America.

New Dawn Enterprises Ltd., located in Sydney, Cape Breton, Nova Scotia, is the oldest and one of the most successful community development corporations in Canada. New Dawn is a third-sector organization,[1] it is distinctive relative to public and private sector organizations in its purpose, configuration and methodology. The organization was incorporated in June, 1976. The vision which underlies its creation is that of a community instrument through which the people can do for themselves. New Dawn's philosophy is grounded in the adult education principles and practices of the Antigonish Movement as established by Moses Coady and Jimmy Tompkins. Their emphasis on the value of co-operation and the potential of each community to determine its economic destiny serve as New Dawn's philosophical anchors.

From the outset, the organization had multiple intentions and thus was attracted to a corporate structure. It chose as its model, however, a different kind of company, a "not-for-profit" corporation, in which the board of directors could not derive material benefit. The directors serve for a limited six-year term and are chosen on the basis of their interest in the welfare of the community and their particular expertise and talents.

The organization set as its aims and objectives its community needs. New Dawn takes pride in the fact that this operating style characterized its first programme. In the late 1970s, a chronic shortage of dentists on Cape Breton Island meant that it was not unusual to wait up to two years for a dental appointment. New Dawn constructed a number of fully-equipped dental clinics, and negotiated with several soon-to-be graduates of the Dalhousie University School of Dentistry to lease and purchase these clinics. The dental project served to set the stage for New Dawn's approach and process: identify the community problem; determine a business-based approach to solve it; do the "deal"; evaluate the results.

Other examples of New Dawn's application of this methodology to community issues include the Cape Breton School of Crafts and half-way houses for the mentally-challenged. New Dawn is best known for its housing projects.

Throughout the 1960s and 1970s, outside consultants, often called in to examine various features of Cape Breton's economic decline, consistently pointed out the poor quality of the housing stock on the Island. After some experimentation, the niche New Dawn identified for itself was that of constructing and operating apartment units. Today, New Dawn is one of the largest private landlords on the Island. Its portfolio consists of more than 250 apartment units and a modest amount of commercial space. Approximately two-thirds of its residential units were built and are operated in co-operation with Canada Mortgage and Housing Corporation. This relationship enables New Dawn to rent units at a price affordable to people receiving a lower-than-average income.

New Dawn's two real estate companies, Cape Breton Association for Housing Development and Pine Tree Park Estates Ltd., are the most visible products of the organization's activities and are its largest asset. In addition, there are currently six other active companies: the New Dawn Guest Home, a thirty-bed residential facility delivering institutional care; Cape Care Services Ltd., which provides in-home for-fee care for seniors; Home Living Ltd., a small-options residential programme for seniors; New Day Ventures Ltd., the construction and maintenance arm of the organization; the Volunteer Resource Centre, which coordinates the work of 300 community volunteers; Highland Resources Ltd., which functions as a registered trade school; and New Dawn itself, the administrative and development sector of the organization. New Dawn consists of two main branches: real estate and health services. Taken together, the companies hold assets valued at $20 million and as of 1996, employ 100 people. Its annual operating budget is more than $4 million.

New Dawn's formation and development were marked by conflict and hardship, as well as occasional triumph. The corporation journeyed through classic development problems: interpersonal conflicts; lack of focus; confusion about priorities; incomplete financial reporting; lack of clarity regarding board versus staff functions; and inadequate budgeting procedures. There were two near-bankruptcies followed by agonizingly slow financial recovery. New Dawn persevered, learning from its mistakes as it gradually developed a capacity for management.

People are usually surprised to discover that New Dawn has received minimal support from government. The exception was a $125,000 demonstration grant from Health and Welfare Canada, awarded in 1978. Despite occasional programme-specific funding, New Dawn has received only monies equally available to the non-profit and private sectors. The Health and Welfare contribution represented the single instance wherein New Dawn received support consistent with its comprehensive development goals.

The New Dawn founders were forced to rely on their creativity and commitment. The down payment for the first building purchased was secured on the basis of a personal guarantee provided by several of the directors. A group of volunteers completed the required renovations. Due to the spirit and perseverance of its founders, the $125,000 provided by Health and Welfare Canada was leveraged into an organization worth $20 million.

Just as the Antigonish Movement is fundamental to understanding the creation of New Dawn, so too are other features of the community's history and culture. Cape Breton's status as an island surrounded by the Atlantic Ocean has shaped in large measure the community's sense of itself.

The Island interested its first European settlers because of the plentiful fish that surrounded its shores. During the first half of the seventeenth century, as Cape Breton was traded between the French and the English, the value of the Island was understood to be the gold of its sea. While for a brief historical moment (1785-1821) the Island was an independent colony, it was ultimately annexed to Nova Scotia. Taken together with Nova Scotia's decision to join Confederation, this meant that the face of Cape Breton was turned away from the sea—inland toward the west.

Early in its history, Cape Breton became an enclave for Scottish Highlanders. The traditions and cultural traits of this immigrant group have dominated the Island's perspective. The geographic and language barriers that characterized their Scottish homeland were largely maintained in the new land; consequently, they were ill-equipped to participate in the industrial transformation on the Island in the late nineteenth century. Prosperity in the new economic order meant creating relationships centred on the practices of commerce, an arrangement uncomfortable for Highlanders who for generations had depended on family and clan for survival. Excluded from the management of companies established to tap the wealth of Cape Breton coal fields, their lot was to supply their labour, and occasionally their lives, for the economic goals of the money barons from "away."

Some hoped that because of the Island's rich natural resources, Cape Breton, would emerge through Confederation as "the national workshop." [2] Instead, once the easily accessible coal was mined, the Island shared the poverty of the Maritime region. Through the 1930s and 1940s, the economic challenge facing the Maritime provinces was taken up by the Premier of Nova Scotia, a native Cape Bretoner, Angus L. MacDonald. On the advice of Harold Innis, the noted University of Toronto scholar, Premier MacDonald advanced the argument that Confederation placed the Maritimes in a peripheral and disadvantaged position.[3] Although MacDonald encountered stiff opposition from the federal government and the wealthier provinces, his persuasive argument helped shape the national system of transfer payments which were institutionalized in the 1950s and 1960s. The Maritimes thus were assured that they would be able to maintain a standard of living well beyond their wealth-generating capacity.

The national prosperity of the late 1950s and the 1960s led to new aspirations by the poorer regions of the country, including Cape Breton. The federal government and the less fortunate provinces embarked on a series of attempts to duplicate the economic activity of southern Ontario. With rare exceptions, these attempts met with disappointing results. For a combination of reasons, Cape Breton was excluded from most of these national programmes; it was subjected instead to a special set of development schemes. Unfortunately, politics always prevailed over sound business judgement. Launched with considerable hype and fanfare, each project eventually crashed against the hard, jagged rocks of reality.

Just as New Dawn has to be understood in the historical context of its community, so too is it informed by Cape Breton culture, especially those aspects which determine economic activity or the lack of it. Alexis de Tocqueville,[4] Edward Banfield,[5] and Jane Jacobs[6] have provided frameworks for understanding the fundamental connection between economic development and culture.

De Tocqueville points to purposeful associations as the strength of a democratic political system. He predicts, however, that governments would find opportunities to discourage the construction of those associations. Once citizens experience government replacing their associations, they lose the notion of working together and so require even more assistance. In Cape Breton the authority of government opinion is as much a part of the Island as the North Atlantic wind: purposeful, community-based, independent associations are rare. New Dawn is just such a rarity. In the context of Cape Breton culture, these traits may be understood as part of its special quality.

Edward Banfield finds the relationship between economic development and a community's capacity to associate and organize fundamental. He points to the propensity to form economic associations beyond family and tribe as the primary feature distinguishing economically-developed from underdeveloped societies. He finds that in communities where attitudes and behaviour mitigate against association, there are no leaders. No one takes the initiative of outlining a course of action and persuading others to embark upon it. If leadership were offered, it would be refused. Cape Breton's economy has more in common with Banfield's conception of third-world societies than with modern Canadian communities. Local leadership is uncommon and viewed with suspicion. New Dawn represents an exception to this dearth of leadership: it is a local initiative following a particular course of action decided upon and implemented by a critical mass of people.

For Jane Jacobs, the link between culture and economic development is subtle. She argues that economies have long been mistaken as national processes. Countries attempt to deal with "their" economies in the same way they deal with political and military issues. An economy should be understood as the function of a city region. A vital city region is one that replaces its imports, a process which leads to patterns of creativity and innovation and, eventually, opportunities for export. In this way economic vitality emerges.

According to Jacobs' analysis, the Canadian economy has only one vital city region, Toronto. Other areas of the country function as supply regions. She thinks Atlantic Canada suffers from the traditional fate of a supply region: the depletion of its resources and the substitution of these resources by other products ensure its continuing decline. Once in decline, a region quickly loses the knowledge which allows self-sufficiency and vitality. The community forfeits its capability and loses all confidence. Jacobs' notion of lost belief could be a portrait of Cape Breton culture.

De Tocqueville, Banfield and Jacobs speak of powerful, implicit connections between the economy of a community and its culture. Undoubtedly Cape Breton's culture is burdened with many of the aforementioned debilities. In part,

New Dawn emerged as a reaction to these cultural traditions. New Dawn stands against the idea of community incompetence. As an expression of the leadership of a critical group of people disproving the notion that the community cannot act co-operatively, New Dawn is an expression of faith challenging the community's lost belief in itself. New Dawn's creation and actions embody an abiding faith in the possibility of the Cape Breton community.

New Dawn is a community economic organization. What this means in the new information-based economy is fundamentally different from its industrial predecessors.[7] While the industrial organization required an authoritarian structure, the modern organization calls for a partnership approach. An information-based economy presumes complexity and specialization, and the application of knowledge to a particular task requires a co-ordinated team effort by a group of well-trained people.

Economic organizations have never been a significant part of the Cape Breton landscape; they are not now. Organizations on the Island, economic or otherwise, are usually based or controlled off-Island. New Dawn, as a locally-based, locally-controlled economic development organization, is a Cape Breton exception.

Although New Dawn frequently describes itself using a corporate model, implying that it is driven by traditional organizational practices, in practice it operates as a team. New Dawn is a volunteer-driven organization. Organizational expertise, especially in project development, is provided by volunteers. New Dawn depends on the effective coordination of the numerous and varied talents of volunteers. An authoritarian model, based on the principles of command and control, wouldn't work in an organization which depends on special skills contributed voluntarily. Volunteers in New Dawn function as associates, not subordinates.

New Dawn is part of a larger community economic development (CED) movement. In Canada, New Dawn was one of the first CED organizations established and has been a model to other groups dealing with communities in decline. The New Dawn founder, Dr. Greg MacLeod, sees New Dawn and other organizations of its kind as motivated by objectives beyond profit. MacLeod[8] argues that the under-development of Cape Breton is attributable to the structural limitations of traditional business enterprise. New Dawn, by contrast, embodies a different structure, one which enables the community to organize its resources effectively to achieve social, cultural and economic growth.

While MacLeod sees New Dawn as a Canadian response to the darker features of private enterprise, the CED movement in the United States is reported to be rooted in the civil rights movement of the 1960s.[9] The violence and destruction of inner city riots led those communities to move from traditional preoccupations with individual rights towards a new sense of group and community responsibility. Whatever the roots of the movements in Canada and the United States, both represent the radical conclusion that poverty and underdevelopment are not the problems of individuals. These are community issues requiring community solutions.

In the past 20 years, the CED movement has attained respectability. Today any activity with a semblance of community representation is called community economic development. However, there are two distinct traditions of CED, the liberal tradition and the progressive tradition.[10] The liberal tradition extends the involvement of the private and public sectors in underdeveloped communities, whereas the progressive tradition judges the established system to be inadequate. The goal of the progressive tradition is to restructure the old order to build new, effective, community-based institutions. New Dawn is preoccupied with re-making the Cape Breton community, taking its place as part of the progressive tradition.

While there are differing points of view about the meaning of community, progressive CED initiatives are grounded in either a common identity or a shared sense of place. New Dawn is anchored by both. The progressive CED model is not only rooted in the concept of community; underlying material objectives is the goal of personal empowerment through community-building. To ensure that CED efforts are humane rather than de-humanizing, they must represent more than material gain. They must serve as instruments to empower their participants and the communities in which they are rooted.

By the fact of its creation in 1976, New Dawn stood against the prevailing belief that the public sector could solve all problems for all people. Twenty years later, New Dawn stands against the conventional idea that the private sector and free-market capitalism will provide the solution to every social and economic problem. New Dawn understands that the complex task of building community is beyond the scope of a one-dimensional approach.

The New Dawn experiment is 20 years old. By any measure, New Dawn is a success—the organization has survived and realized a significant number of achievements. For its members, New Dawn's twenty-year journey is but a beginning. New Dawn's members intend this experiment to continue for another twenty years, and then twenty more, probing, searching, and deal-making, for the New Dawn mission is "establishing and operating ventures that contribute to the creation of a self-supporting community."[11]

This chapter was previously published in *Community Economic Development: In Search of Empowerment*. Eric Schragge, ed. Montréal: Black Rose Books, 1997.

Reprinted by permission.

ENDNOTES

1. As opposed to private or public sectors.

2. T.W. Acheson, "The National Policy and the Industrialisation of the Maritimes, 1880-1990" in P. Bucker and D. Frank (Eds.), *The Acadiensis Reader, Volume 2, Atlantic Canada After Confederation.* Fredericton: Acadiensis Press, 1985.

3. J. Bickerton, *Nova Scotia, Ottawa and the Politics of Regional Development.* Toronto: University of Toronto Press, 1990.

4. Alexis de Toqueville, *Democracy in America.* New York: The New American Library, 1956.

5. E. Banfield, *The Moral Basis of a Backward Society.* New York: The Free Press, 1958.

6. Jane Jacobs, *Cities and the Wealth of Nations: Principles of Economic Life.* New York: Random House, 1984.

7. Peter Drucker, *Post-Capitalist Society.* New York: Harper-Collins, 1993.

8. Greg MacLeod, *New Age Business: Community Corporations that Work.* Ottawa: Canadian Council on Social Development, 1986.

9. S. Perry, *Communities on the Way: Rebuilding Local Economies in the United States and Canada.* Albany: State University of New York Press, 1997.

10. J. Fontan, *A Critical Review of Canadian, American, and European Community Economic Development Literature.* Vancouver: Centre for Community Enterprise, 1993.

11. New Dawn Mission Statement.

5

FINANCING VENTURES IN A DEPLETED COMMUNITY

HARVEY JOHNSTONE

The importance of small and medium-sized enterprises to the Canadian economy is well-established. In the late 1980s, 47 percent of all working Canadians were employed in firms with fewer than 100 employees whereas small firms accounted for 29 percent of all business sales. Between 1979 and 1989, small firms with fewer than 50 employees created 81 percent of all net new jobs in Canada—a total of 2.1 million jobs.[1] Similar levels of performance have been observed in other industrialized countries.[2]

Partly as a consequence of this new prominence, issues related to small-firm sector financing have also assumed greater importance in recent years. In particular, considerable research effort has been focused on issues such as new venture finance and finance of the initial stages of growth in small firms. Recent studies and commentaries indicate that traditional sources of finance may not be adequate in meeting the full spectrum of small-firm needs. Studies conducted for the British Department of Employment show that banks there are reluctant to finance individuals attempting to start businesses for the purposes of self-employment.[3]

The Canadian banking industry's hesitation to lend money to small firms has prompted the Federal Minister of Small

Business, Tom Hockin, to modify the *Small Business Loans Act*. Now, banks can charge higher rates of interest on government-guaranteed loans.[4] In 1992, small business loans made by the big six banks had dropped four billion dollars from 1989 levels. The lack of response by Canadian banks is seen both as a barrier to entry for potential new small firms and as a barrier to growth for existing ones.

Shortcomings in the finance/capital industry are not limited to the banks. International evidence indicates shortages in long-term investment financing (particularly for start-up and initial growth). Moreover, this "equity gap" has occurred at a time when the institutional venture-capital industry was actually expanding.[5] The perception of several unfilled niches in Canada's capital/finance industry has led MPs in Ottawa to seek policy changes promoting alternatives to bank financing; such alternatives would include trust companies, credit unions and leasing companies.[6]

Unfortunately, filling the niches is not a simple task. In this complex industry, good intentions are no substitute for well-designed policies. The manner in which Canadian banks have used the *Small Business Loans Act* has come under criticism recently from the Federation of Independent Business. Federation President John Bulloch has argued that the banks have used government guarantees to secure their positions with clients who would have been served even if the *Small Business Loans Act* didn't exist. From Bulloch's perspective, the Small Business Loans Act programme was functioning as a "loan-subsidy program for the banks."

A more responsive banking industry may not be the answer, however. Barclays Bank, the United Kingdom's largest small-firm lender, reported average small-firm loan write-offs of $18 million per week in 1992. In response to pressure, the bank funded numerous small-firm ventures; by the early 1990s, many of these firms were economically marginal, inadequately managed and financially vulnerable.[7] Current structures may be incapable of responding adequately to perceived needs; contemporary commentary suggests that present and traditional financial practices are inadequate for the needs of small firms. If legitimate, these criticisms imply that a series of niches or gaps exist, in which genuine needs go unmet. Importantly, these critiques also imply that those needs can be met within the bounds of good business principles. These claims are substantiated by presenting the case of a locally spawned community financial institution in Cape Breton and two of its client firms.

Existing financial institutions had failed these client companies, East Coast Rope and A&B Mechanical. The nature of these failures was important. They were not merely cases of oversight: the failure was systemic. Companies like these are beyond the scope of normal operations of traditional financial institutions; they occupy a niche in which an alternative financial institution is required, such as the BCA group of companies. BCA can provide for this niche because of its unique operating principles and legal structure, which render it logically distinct from existing institutions. BCA is bound nonetheless by the principles of good business (confirmed by its survival in the market place) and by its perspective on risk.

East Coast Rope is based in North Sydney and employs approximately 30 people. In May of 1992, the Canadian Imperial Bank of Commerce called in an operating loan from Scotia Ropes, a high-tech, government-backed rope manufacturing company in North Sydney. This precipitated a number of events, including an attempt to dispose of Scotia Ropes' highly specialized machinery. A Louisiana-based company expressed interest in acquiring and removing the assets. News of this contemplated action triggered enormous community support to keep the machinery in Cape Breton. With BCA's leadership, the machinery of the bankrupt Scotia Rope Company was acquired by the newly formed East Coast Rope.

A plumbing and heating company based in Sydney had 19 employees. This old established company was going bankrupt. The unemployed workers attempted to reconstitute the company but the banks had refused financing. BCA provided friendly capital, and the workers began to operate under a new name, A&B Mechanical.

Located in Cape Breton Island, BCA refers to a complex of companies which takes an innovative and experimental approach to local economic development. In Atlantic Canada, governments have used a variety of unsuccessful techniques to attract businesses but there have been many reports of government money wasted in fruitless subsidies in all parts of Canada, not just this one. Additionally, not every constituency within the Atlantic region can be considered depleted. There are pockets of prosperity such as Halifax and Moncton where unemployment levels are well below the national average. For most of Atlantic Canada, however, the challenge is to make businesses successful in depleted and beleaguered economies.

BCA can be classed as a community venture-finance company. It is an experiment in local economic development. Legally, BCA Holdings Limited is a corporation incorporated under the *Companies Act of Nova Scotia*, and is limited by guarantee. This means that it is a not-for-profit company established for a public purpose rather than a regular share-capital company with a private purpose. BCA Holdings is actually the umbrella organization for a group of community-oriented companies. Some of these are conventional share-capital companies; others are not-for-profit corporations. The key subsidiary company is BCA Venture Capital Limited. Both BCA Holdings Ltd. and BCA Venture Capital Ltd. can lend to or purchase shares in other companies.

BCA began as a committee set up by the Community Economic Development Institute at University College of Cape

Breton (UCCB). It is an experimental corporation, considered to be part of what is called the community business sector. These kinds of businesses are amalgams: they try to combine the best from regular corporate commerce with that from community development and the co-operative movements. Other firms in the community business sector include GNP Development Corp., based in Newfoundland, and New Dawn Enterprises, which is based in Cape Breton. New Dawn is involved in housing and has assets of over $20 million; it has operated since the mid-1970s.

Perhaps the best example of community business enterprises can be found in the Basque region of Spain. The Mondragon Co-operative Corporation is worker-owned and is dedicated to the social and economic development of the Basque area.[8] Employing 24,000 workers, Mondragon competes successfully in international markets, producing stoves, refrigerators, furniture and factory machinery (including robots). Its annual sales total more than $3 billion. The Mondragon co-operative operates a highly successful banking system that finances much of the industrial complex. In Québec, a union-based fund called *Solidarité* assists Québec-based enterprises. Examples such as these indicate that community businesses could not flourish without developing an allied financial institution.

BCA tried several such alliances before a solution was found, first with League Savings and Mortgage based in Halifax and, later, with Co-Operators Insurance, of Guelph, Ontario. These attempted partnerships did not work. Finally, BCA decided to incorporate its own finance company and proceeded to look for money. Wide consultation among lawyers, accountants and business leaders helped formulate the growing BCA idea.

In 1990, the group was presented with a great opportunity. Enterprise Cape Breton had offered an interest-free loan of $500,000 to the Industrial Cape Breton Board of Trade to be used as a venture development fund, if the Board could match that amount. The Board of Trade declined, stating that it was outside their mandate. BCA took up the challenge. Enterprise Cape Breton set out a condition that BCA would have to raise its share within six months to access the interest-free loan. Since BCA was not listed as a public company and had not prepared a prospectus (a prohibitively expensive undertaking), the group could not advertise publicly. Word was spread through the informal network. BCA made presentations to organizations such as the Kiwanis Club and the Professional Women's Association. People were buttonholed on the street and invited to invest.[9] There was also strong support from the clergy, who understood immediately that money could be directed according to ethical community principles. A Toronto-based church group called the Canadian Alternative Investment Co-operative agreed to lend money if backed by a mortgage on real property. To strengthen the portfolio, both New Dawn Enterprises and New Deal Development Corporation provided loan guarantees to BCA. Within six months, BCA raised more than $500,000 in the local community and commenced negotiations with Enterprise Cape Breton.

The negotiations proved to be an extremely complicated process, involving two law firms and an accounting company over several months. In the meantime, the investors in BCA met and confirmed the initial board. During this period, the organizers kept in close contact with the Nova Scotia Securities Commission, which provided useful guidance. The government development agencies were perplexed to be dealing with an investment company which was not mainly motivated by profit maximization.

Both BCA Holdings Ltd., the parent corporation, and BCA Ventures Capital Ltd., its principal subsidiary, make loans and buy shares. A common board and a single staff manage the companies. The three main criteria for investment are these:

1. The company must be viable commercially;

2. The company must serve the local community good in some way;

3. The company must be locally owned and controlled, and must have more than one owner.

BCA's investment strategy is conservative: the majority of investment is secured by real property. As a general rule, only investments over $75,000 are considered, since other community agencies service small-scale loans. A policy committee, chosen at an annual meeting of investors, develops policy guidelines which guide the Board of Directors. By design, the Board of Directors of BCA includes both community leaders and business experts.

From the point of view of most operations, BCA is similar to a conventional business; it must generate money for expenses, deal with management, and solve problems like any other company. It is profoundly different in other senses:

1. BCA's prime motivation is community improvement; profit is a means, not an end in itself;

2. It is not owned by shareholders; it operates as a trust in local community interests;

3. BCA is localized and builds on the local community; it cannot be "bought-out;"

4. It depends upon a high degree of volunteer involvement.

Business corporations did not start with Henry Ford. Two of the oldest business corporations in the western world operate in Cape Breton today: the Hudson's Bay Company, incorporated in 1670, and Stora Koppaberg, incorporated in the 14th century. A corporation is a group of individuals who are given the legal privilege of acting as one individual. Such a privilege was granted by kings to those who performed special services for the kingdom, such as the Hudson's Bay company which had extended the British Empire and, at times, had governed in the name of the Crown. In the 19th century, John Stuart Mill argued against the parliamentary practice of granting limited liability to corporations, pointing out that limited liability favoured a few individuals instead of serving the interests of the nation. He held the view that business corporations should have a public trust. However, the legal tradition in the United States considers corporations as entities free to act as private persons.

BCA's position is that a business corporation is not simply a private entity; the corporation as a collective entity can be considered to be a kind of public person. It exists through legal and public privilege and, therefore, has social obligations. These go beyond the simple commitment to respect the laws of the land. Every business corporation, by its nature, has a responsibility to serve the public purpose. One implication of this position is that managers are bound by much more than an obligation to serve the shareholders; their primary obligation is to serve the public. Thus, managers must respect the environment, enhance the quality of work life for employees and attend to the needs of local society. It is a distortion for managers to claim accountability only to shareholders. As L.C. Gower, in his classic textbook on modern company law points out, the modern shareholder is a moneylender to a corporation rather than its owner.[10] Many legal commentators recognize that ownership by the shareholders is, in most cases, a legal fiction. Law usually lags behind reality, often taking considerable time to reflect it. Gower, like others, calls for a radical revision of company law.

Current economic thinking is centred on mechanical, quantitative measures of performance. The fate of individuals as a result of commercial decisions is considered to be an external. Quality of life and job security do not appear on balance sheets and profit and loss statements. BCA has shown that economics and business activity can be conducted in terms of persons and communities. The choice to conceive of business from the perspective of human welfare, or merely in terms of financial return, is determined by the view of business as a means or as an end. In the mechanistic paradigm, profit is the goal; good works in the community are merely a way to improve public relations and increase revenue. In the humanistic paradigm, community well-being is at stake and profits are used as a means to achieve it. In both cases, profits must be made but the rationale is different. This makes an enormous difference in corporate behaviour, affecting such decisions as where a company is located and the degree of quality in the product.

A frequent criticism of the modern business corporation is that, being self-contained, it has no loyalty to any one community. At first, national corporations developed; more recently, multinational or international corporations move from country to country, subject to no one particular government. A community business corporation, however, is rooted in a particular geographic location and is resistant to buy-outs from outside corporations.

Debates rage on the question of whether business corporations so connected to a particular geographic area can be competitive. Most large corporations vigorously oppose such an idea in the interests of business flexibility. Corporations like Mondragon in Spain, and smaller ones like New Dawn and BCA, refute the notion that successful corporations must be place-neutral. Alternative structures such as these raise a host of theoretical questions, threatening conventional business wisdom.

Conventional business measures in terms of real-world success or failure. By this criterion, the client companies of BCA, initially refused by the banks, are thriving. In 1995, East Coast Rope exceeded all expectations, selling 35 percent of its polysteel rope on the Pacific coast. Unable to keep up with demand for its high quality product, the company purchased new machinery and expanded its capacity in the summer of 1995. Management standards are met with the high quality and strength of the rope being produced. More than 30 people are being employed on a round-the-clock basis. A strong relationship with UCCB has helped to implement a strong research and development programme to create alternative products. The company is considering new product lines based upon high-strength fiber production. East Coast Rope registered a profit in 1995 and has continued to grow; BCA Holdings is the largest single shareholder. Since 1993, A&B Mechanical has steadily improved its sales by winning competitive tendered contracts. This year the company has won industrial plumbing and heating bids as far away as Antigonish, in mainland Nova Scotia. A&B Mechanical is diversifying into commercial building maintenance. Recently, it won a competitive maintenance tender for a major commercial building in the area. In 1995, A&B Mechanical registered a profit and employed 25 people. It continues to prosper today.

In addition to these companies, BCA has had other successes: the Bras d'Or Lakes Inn in St. Peters (formerly the bankrupt Inn on the Canal); the Tompkins Commercial Centre in Reserve Mines; a local radio station (CHER) and a company which manufactures cement blocks. BCA has more than one million dollars in investments and controls close to five million in assets.

BCA's organizational structure is no magic solution to Cape Breton's tough economic problems. Because BCA uses community-based venture capital (often from novice investors), it is particularly susceptible to criticism if it fails. The risks are higher for BCA than for a conventional financial institution, especially as it invests in businesses operating in a depleted community. The retail market in Cape Breton is more than 20 percent below the national average; thus, BCA also risks criticism for investing in projects refused by investment experts.

It is incumbent upon a community-based venture-capital company to devise risk management strategies. BCA's strategic approach is to involve experts in the management of its fledgling firms. For example, the CHER radio investment involves a partner with a proven record in the communications industry. His input has been critically important in repositioning the station and capturing a larger share of the listening audience. Similarly, East Coast Rope's recovery is due, in large measure, to the involvement of an investor with exceptional expertise in rope manufacture; he has reorganized production processes and quality control more efficiently.

Often, business failure can be traced back to weaknesses in management skills. Many of the projects in which BCA has invested lacked management expertise. Where highly-specialized knowledge was needed, BCA's strategy has been to identify and enlist experts to reduce risk.

BCA's approach is not new. A recent study of private investors in the United Kingdom indicates that private UK investors usually have a particular form of expertise. Many of them are or have been professional managers. When they invest, they choose projects in industrial sectors that are familiar to them. Not only do they provide the target firm with much needed capital, they provide it with management expertise as well, taking a hands-on approach. As private investors, they value their anonymity; to preserve it, they tend to operate in small groups or networks of like-minded individuals. These networks are used for referrals. Typically, private investors are passive. They are not prospectors; they tend to wait for investment projects to find them. Like BCA, UK private investors invest locally (within a 50-mile radius of their homes). Research shows that they may refuse as many as 92 percent of the opportunities referred to them. In large measure, the high refusal rate reflects their insistence on backing only local projects within their field of expertise.

While similarities exist between these private investors and the approach taken by BCA, there are important differences, too. Compared to UK private investors, BCA has invested in a much higher percentage of the projects referred to it. What is more disturbing is the diversity of projects in BCA's portfolio: a hotel, a rope manufacturer, a ski hill, a radio station, a plumbing contractor, a commercial centre. If risk is to be reduced through management expertise, BCA has no choice but to enlist outside experts and entice them to become involved. Thus, a crucial difference between the strategies of UK private investors and BCA is this: BCA does not rely on resident expertise, choosing instead to recruit partners with appropriate expertise into joint ventures. In this way, BCA can accept more locally-based opportunities referred to it.

BCA's portfolio differs in other ways from the typical private investor's portfolio. Most of BCA's client firms are older businesses; some have been operating for several decades. This is an important point, because research indicates that firms are most likely to grow when young. In general, there is a four-year incubation period, followed by two years of sharp growth and steady growth thereafter. Growing firms have much higher rates of survival compared to those that don't grow, although older firms have higher survival rates than young firms. This suggests that many of BCA's client firms are unlikely to grow significantly, the one exception being East Coast Rope. As a consequence, most of BCA's investments are unlikely to provide high rates of return to its investors. Under good management, however, the firms in

BCA's portfolio should have reasonably good prospects for a prolonged life.

Most private investors report that they would have invested more if they had come across a greater number of suitable investment opportunities.[11] In other words, these private investors needed an improved deal-flow. By marked contrast to this, BCA has already invested most of its resources. Such divergence may raise concerns about BCA's approach: is BCA selective enough?

BCA has extended its reach beyond the financial function. Perhaps it is better to describe BCA as a financial management company; thus, the high levels of risk associated with businesses operating in a depleted community can be reduced to tolerable levels. BCA could take on a new role: with much of its own resources already invested, BCA may act as a referral service to other investors. Alternatively, BCA could seek new sources of investment capital in order to expand its own portfolio.

Although no strategic decision has been taken, BCA needs to develop a focus for future investments. Despite the depletion of the local economy, there are many small firms in the advanced technology and entertainment sectors. Many of these young firms have significant growth potential. Focusing on this sector may help BCA to further reduce its risk while providing opportunities for strong growth in the future.

BCA represents an innovative and logically distinct business entity in the finance-capital industry. This new form of company is able to serve a broad clientele, including those companies whose needs would not be met by traditional financial institutions.

ENDNOTES

1. Yvonne Gasse, "Importance of the Small and Medium-sized Enterprise in the Canadian Economy" in *Journal of Small Business and Entrepreneurship*, Vol. 11, No. 3, 1994.

2. D.J. Storey and S.G. Johnson, *Job Creation in Small and Medium-Sized Enterprises, Commission of the European Communities, Vol. 1*. Newcastle: Centre for Urban and Regional Development Studies, University of Newcastle-Upon-Tyne, 1987; D. Birch, *The Job Generation Process*. Cambridge, Massachusetts: Massachusetts Institute of Technology Program On Neighborhood and Regional Change, 1979; and D. Birch, *Job Creation in America: How Our Smallest Companies Put The Most People To Work*. New York: The Free Press, 1987.

3. Julie Bevan, "Barriers to Business Start-up: A Study of the Flow Into and Out of Self-Employment," Research Paper No. 71, Department of Employment, HMSO, United Kingdom, 1989.

4. "Recession-Burned Banks More Hesitant To Lend." *Globe and Mail*, February 8, 1993, p. B6.

5. Colin Mason and Richard Harrison, "Closing the Regional Equity Gap: The Role of Informal Venture Capital," in *Small Business Economics*, Vol. 7, No. 2, 1995.

6. "Banks Should Assist Small Business, MPs Say." *The Globe and Mail*, December 5, 1994, page B6.

7. "Shop of Little Horrors," *The Economist*, Nov. 13, 1993, pp. 83-84.

8. Greg MacLeod, *New Age Business: Community Corporations That Work*. Ottawa: Canadian Council on Social Development, 1986.

9. A interesting insight was gained through this process. Of those approached, women responded differently from men. Men normally asked, "What is the rate of return?" The answer was five per cent. The typical reply was, "I get twenty percent in the Alligator Fund which is big in Afghanistan." Women wanted to know "What are you going to do with the money?" Told that BCA was trying to build a commercial building in Reserve Mines, or reopen a closed company, the usual response was to transfer money from a conventional savings account into BCA.

10. L.C.B. Gower, *The Principles of Modern Company Law*. London: Stevens and Sons, 1969.

11. Colin Mason and Richard Harrison, "Strategies for Expanding the Informal Venture Capital Market," in *International Small Business Journal*, Vol. 2, No. 4, 1993, pp. 23-38.

6

THE MIRA PASTURE CO-OPERATIVE
CHARLES MACDONALD

The Mira Pasture Co-operative is a community development project that has not been described previously in the growing literature on community economic development in Cape Breton. Its beginnings, like those of New Dawn Enterprises Limited, go back to the mid-1970s, when many new initiatives were undertaken to address the economic and social problems facing Cape Breton Island. New Dawn Enterprises started in the urban environment of Sydney, Nova Scotia, and took on the challenge of providing affordable housing; the Mira Pasture Co-operative had its roots in rural Cape Breton, and tackled the problem of the decline of agriculture.

This chapter presents the story of the Mira Pasture Co-op, a story whose most significant chapters were written back in colonial Cape Breton, in the decline of agricultural activity after World War II, and in the days of the emerging co-op, in the mid-1970s.

In the fall of 1973, five men met to assess the future of farming along the Mira River in Cape Breton. Three were self-employed, one was a school bus-driver, the fifth a young university lecturer. The university lecturer was meeting three of the other men for the first time; all of the others were long-time friends and neighbours. They were linked by a common interest in their community and a desire to improve the prospects for farming along the Mira River.

The conversation that evening set in motion a series of community meetings, during which increasing numbers of committed individuals grew in their understanding of the history of farming along the Mira. They came also to a common assessment of what had caused the situation they faced. The story of their project is instructive, exemplifying as it does the dynamics of community economic development. Their experience shows that a project rooted in a community and embraced by committed people willing to pool their knowledge and resources has a good chance of survival. It illustrates also the importance of co-operating with political leaders and government resource people. And it demonstrates the power of wedding traditional knowledge to willingness to adapt.

Local people refer to the Mira as a river. In reality, it might be better described as a series of lakes strung out in a line that runs about 35 miles through the southeastern part of Cape Breton, emptying finally into the Atlantic Ocean. As early as the 1700s (the period of the French settlement), farming thrived along the sloping banks of the river. The French recognized the richness of the land. They were particularly impressed with its capacity to produce excellent grasses for pasture, and they believed they could grow several varieties of grain in the area as well.

After the Fall of Louisbourg in 1759, most of the land that French settlers had cleared was abandoned. The land remained uncultivated until the various waves of Scottish immigrants arrived, beginning at the end of the 18th century and continuing into the first half of the 19th century. Interestingly, the early Scottish immigrants were the forebears of at least four of the five men who met that evening in 1974.

All of the men who met that evening, and the many who joined them over the next few years, had first-hand experience of the fertility of the Mira. Born in the 1920s and 1930s, they had worked on their parents' farmsteads. Though those farms were essentially mixed farming operations, most had a small herd of dairy cows as mainstay to produce milk, cream and butter. Each had a small flock of sheep, usually around 40 head. And they produced vegetables, mostly for home consumption, although surpluses would be sold off-farm. Income was supplanted seasonally, by work in road maintenance and from the sale of modest amounts of timber bought by the Dominion Iron and Steel Company for use in the coal mines of Cape Breton. Each farm's main cash flow came from the sale of milk to dairies located in Sydney, about 17 miles from the Mira.

After World War II, there were more than 40 producers in Mira shipping milk to Sydney. By the mid-60s, that number had dwindled to one. Rural electrification, replacement of farm animals by machines and motorization of transportation had within the space of 20 years, drastically changed farming.

Until electrification, all of the dairy operations were modest; very few farmers had more than 20 producing animals. Milking was done by hand, and each day's milk was kept cool during the summer in a dug-out basement or well, or in an ice-box filled with ice collected in winter from frozen lakes. The eight gallon cans of milk were collected by the milk truck every other day and delivered to the dairies in Sydney.

With rural electrification came mechanical milking machines, and an even more formidable advance—the bulk tank. Instead of shipping their milk in cans which could easily be handled by a single person, farmers stored it in much larger, electrically-powered coolers. The milk was pumped for transport into a tanker truck, which moved from farm to farm.

That technology radically changed the business of shipping milk. Producers had to buy into the new system or arrange for the private transportation of their milk in traditional containers to the dairy. Earlier, the milk-man called at all farms, small and large to pick up milk cans, but the truck had to be operated more economically. Small farmers, unwilling or unable to buy a bulk tank, were left off the truck's route and so were soon out of business.

Within a few years, economics forced even the larger operators to stop dairy farming. By the late 1970s, not a drop of milk was being shipped from the Mira. Gradually, cows disappeared from the farms, and farmers, though they had the skills and the land for farming, had to work for wages in the steel mill, the construction industry or in forestry.

Another radical shift in farming practices came in the summer foraging of cattle. The animals would be turned out morning and evening to wend their way along the roads, searching for fresh forage in the meadows and on vacant farms. Only in late fall, after the hay was harvested and the aftergrass had grown, were the animals allowed back on the fields. This custom disappeared with the motorization of the countryside. Animals posed a danger to the motoring public; they were also unwelcome to the increasing number of cottagers whose properties dotted the banks of the Mira. Farmers had to choose: keep their animals by developing pasture lands and surrounding them with sturdy fencing, or sell off their animals and let the fields lie fallow.

Modernization forever changed farming along the Mira and throughout rural Nova Scotia. The men from the Mira knew that modernization made it impossible for them to return to the farming practices of the past. Yet they wanted to farm and they wanted to restore agriculture to their community.

The Mira farmers decided to develop a community pasture. The concept was an ancient one: local farmers were given the option of taking their animals to a central foraging area for the summer. The grassland would be fenced and supervised, and the carrying capacity of the pasture continuously improved through modern land management methods. Participants would be charged, per annum for the service. The community pasture meant several important benefits: home fields could be dedicated to the production of hay for use over the winter months; individual farmers would be spared the major expense of fencing their own properties; and they would be freed from daily managing their animals during the busy summer season. All were substantial benefits for part-time farmers holding full-time jobs away from their homes.

The Mira farmers were familiar with the community pasture concept; in fact, they had urged the local governing body, the Cape Breton County Council, to take the lead in developing such a service. The Council did strike a committee for this purpose in the late 1960s, but made no progress on the project. Despite the delay, the farmers did not abandon the idea. They knew that the Nova Scotia Department of Agriculture developed community pastures throughout the province. They had visited one such pasture, in Mabou, about 80 miles from the Mira. The Mabou pasture was what they envisioned for their own land. In fact, some farmers in Cape Breton County long used the Mabou Pasture. By the early 1970s, the Mabou Pasture was filled to capacity, so the Mira group decided to develop their own.

The fact that the Nova Scotia government had by then lost interest in developing community pastures did not deter the Mira group. After many meetings, they decided to incorporate their group under the provisions of the *Co-operatives Act of Nova Scotia*. On the third of March, 1977, the Mira Pasture Co-operative was born. To assure that members were serious participants and to get some working capital, the membership fee was set at one hundred dollars per share, each member being limited to buying five shares and having one vote. Approximately 30 people had participated in some of the preliminary general meetings. After several years of operation, the membership settled at 25, and a resolution was passed to limit the membership to that number.

As a registered co-operative, the Pasture group was responsible to the Inspector of Co-operatives of Nova Scotia, to whom the group had to forward annual financial statements to retain its status under Nova Scotia law. Since its inception, the Mira Group has been led by an active executive committee, which has maintained a very close liaison with the two managers who have served the Co-op over the years. The group has bypassed the customary co-operative practice of electing a board of directors. Instead, it prefers to have frequent meetings of the small general membership to discuss the group business. As a rule, the group meets formally at least four times each year. The activities of the Co-op are entrusted to several committees who work closely with the manager.

In the beginning, the Co-op's most important committee was the Land Committee that oversaw acquisition of land, clarification of titles, and supervision of extensive surveys of the properties. The Cattle Committee undertook to assist the manager in the operation of the pasture each year. Questions such as stocking rates, pasture fees, setting and enforcing regulations for pasture animals, and determining the dates for opening and closing the pasture came under the purview of the Cattle Committee. A Social Committee established at the outset, was charged with the responsibility for fundraising activities, like the Blueberry Festival, an annual event since 1982.

Over the past 25 years, the Mira Pasture Co-op has demonstrated its philosophy of community economic development through creative acquisition of capital, progressive animal husbandry and commitment to the welfare of the communities along the Mira River.

Building up the capital requirements of the Co-op, in particular land, was one of the first challenges. The site selected for the pasture was at Big Ridge, on the south side of the River at Marion Bridge. This site is central, has land for expansion, and it had been farmed in the early years of the century. What is more, the land had been lumbered, after which a devastating fire in 1976 had destroyed or damaged most of the remaining wood. The logging and the fire prepared the way for the land to be cleared for agricultural use again.

But how did the group of 25 members get the money to acquire and develop their target of one thousand acres? The share capital they raised was the start, but other important factors came into play. For example, members used family connections to acquire the land at preferential prices. In most instances, the vendor was an older relative of a group member, someone no longer interested in developing the land. Some owners had left the area and were living in the United States. At their own expense, members of the Co-op took it upon themselves to visit those owners to negotiate favourable prices. With some owners, the Co-op agreed to restrictive covenants which would apply if the land was ever sold.

The Co-op also acquired some Crown land, property owned by the Province of Nova Scotia. Very early, it was clear that one piece of Crown land would be crucial to the Co-op. Since the Crown would not sell the land, the Co-op enlisted the help of the Cape Breton County Council to acquire it. To do so, the Co-op bought a piece of land from the County, and gave it to the province in exchange for the land it needed.

Co-op members acquired the cash to buy land by the creative use of the wood that was essentially waste material on the property. The trees that had been burned extensively in the fire of 1976 proved to be marketable firewood. Some timber was used to construct two buildings on the property—a pole barn for storing hay and equipment, and a log cabin, which served as meeting place for the Co-op members and eventually as a social centre. Other early sources of cash were a gravel pit on the land, and an arrangement with the Crown that permitted Co-op members to harvest and sell firewood from neighbouring Crown lands.

Members' resourcefulness assured development of the property as well. "Sweat equity," the volunteered services of the members, was the determining factor in developing the agricultural potential of the property. Members put their labour and their machinery at the Co-op's disposal in the early years. Developing the pasture, fencing more than 250 acres, and planting the first fields, were all accomplished by the members themselves.

The federal and provincial governments also contributed significantly to the Pasture. For years the Co-op used government programmes for land-clearing and development as well as a variety of make-work programmes to clear and seed more than a quarter of their holdings. Once the land was developed for forage and the pasture opened for grazing, the Co-op used its user-fees to pay many of the operating costs.

The Co-op's husbandry practices changed significantly over the life of the project. All of the members had been exposed to dairy farming, and many were familiar with the care and management of sheep. The members were not, however, beef farmers, yet early on, they realized that improving breeding stock and grazing animals efficiently and productively had to become important targets for the group.

An interesting part of the early Co-op experience was the establishment of rules for grazing animals on the pasture. All members were extremely attentive to the condition of animals coming onto the site in order to avoid diseases. General rules were established very quickly: animals had to be inoculated and have their horns removed well in advance of admission to the field, and the number of animals grazing on the common pasture, was limited. Limited access was also possible for non-members.

Steps were then taken to improve the genetic quality of the animals. Over the life of the project (nearly 20 years in 1997), purebred bulls had been used. They made for a noticeable improvement in the quality of the stock. The Provincial Department of Agriculture helped by supplying a variety of purebred bulls over the years.

A significant development during the past 20 years was the change in management of the fields. During the first two years, animals were turned loose to graze at will over the entire pasture. In principal, this free-range grazing was no different from the traditional practice of turning animals out to find their own forage. They were free to eat whatever grasses they found most palatable, leaving aside less savory species, which quickly became overripe and even unpalatable. Then in the early 1980s, the Co-op experimented with division of the fields. They rotated animals among four fields, forcing them to consume all of the forage in one section before they were moved to a new one. Though progressive, the plan proved ineffective because the Pasture's electric fencing was inadequate to confine the animals. Ten years later, the Federal Department of Agriculture made it possible to try the system again. Nine separate paddocks were created with the most advanced of electric fencing. The result was higher average weight gains and a longer pasture season.

The social element of Co-op membership has always been of prime importance. All executive meetings are held in the homes of the members, where social graces, such as good conversation and hospitality, have played a very important role. Regular meetings of the group were prefaced by extended conversation about community developments and news. The facilities of the Co-op, especially the log cabin, has been open to community groups and community socials. A new challenge for the Co-op arose in the Spring of 1997 when its log cabin, long its centre of activity, was destroyed by fire. The entire membership rallied to make plans for speedy replacement of this facility.

The Co-op's hospitality has also been extended to government representatives. They have regularly been invited to view the project. An outstanding example of the Co-op's hospitality was the hosting of the annual national board meeting of *Katimavik* in the early 1980s. This national exchange programme, initiated by the Canadian government as a kind of home-grown Peace Corps, had undertaken projects all across Canada. With this gesture, The Mira Pasture Co-op established itself as one of the longest-standing sponsors of the Katimavik programme.

And the Co-op has created jobs in the community. Work on the pasture has been an important element in the domestic finances of many members of the area. University students had summer jobs on the project. The Co-op's policy is to give job priority to needy families. Workers, especially the young, have, in doing meaningful and creative manual labour, developed pride in the project and confidence in their own competence.

The Mira Pasture Co-op contains some lessons for rural community economic development. Connection to a supportive community has been crucial. Co-op members were committed to improving the community in which they lived. They wanted to use local resources, whether land, skills, machinery or buildings. The community recognized the value of the project and benefitted from it, in that the Co-op enhanced social life, made jobs and added an important piece of agricultural infrastructure to the local area.

Another important factor for the success of the group was the presence of self-employed members who provided leadership during the early years of the project. They were resourceful and had experience in dealing with business people, employees and government agencies.

Its connection to the University College of Cape Breton was also very important to the group. Just as New Dawn Enterprises had received much of its early direction from UCCB, so also did the Co-op; in fact, three members were UCCB faculty members. Their skill in research, advocacy, and government relations had a great impact on group decision-making. Interestingly, when the five founding members were ready to present their plans to a wider group, they insisted on having their first meetings at the University.

Educating the membership was crucial to the progress of the Co-op. Resource people from the University and the provincial Department of Agriculture have been regular speakers, on topics like crop rotation, alternative grazing systems, animal husbandry, water supply systems, and irrigation.

Much of the success of the Mira Pasture Co-op is difficult to measure, especially the personal growth of the members and the spirit of pride generated in the community. But the pasture itself stands as a visible sign of the group's achievement: more than 1,000 acres acquired, 25 cleared in 1979, and by 1997, 250 ready for grazing. Good management has extended the grazing period from 79 days to more than 130, and the grazing herd has grown from 79 head to more than 200.

New members have joined the Co-op, and gradually, the challenge of carrying the project forward has passed to new hands. As the Mira Pasture Co-op approaches its third decade of existence, its members recognize that the sustainability is linked to a new challenge, building markets for their beef on Cape Breton Island. As they face this new task, the Co-op members will stay faithful to the principles that gave birth to their project: community rootedness; entrepreneurial imagination; the university connection; and the continuing education of the membership.

7

THE SURVIVAL OF A SMALL COMMUNITY
KAREN MALCOLM

Isle Madame lies at the southeastern tip of Cape Breton, at the mouth of the Strait of Canso, on Chedabucto Bay. The Island is about 12 kilometres wide and 18 kilometres long, the population of 4,300 is about 70 percent bilingual Acadian. The people of the Island live in a number of small rural and coastal communities and four larger ones, West Arichat, Arichat, Petit de Grat and D'Escousse. Four decades ago, the people of Isle Madame were largely self-sufficient. But over the past two decades, there has been increasing economic leakage from the Island to Port Hawkesbury, a commercial centre a half-hour drive away.

Fish brought Acadian and Irish settlers to Isle Madame and since the 18th century, fishing has been the mainstay of the economy. Over the past two decades, fish catches have slowly declined, as has the Island's population. The closure of the ground fishery in 1994 virtually wiped out the basis of the economy; the Richmond Fisheries plant in D'Escousse has been demolished. Lobster and scallop fishing continue, but they too are in decline.

The people of Isle Madame were determined that their community would survive. Isle Madame's situation is similar to that of many communities in Atlantic Canada whose economy and lifestyle relied upon fishing and who never diversified beyond fishing. The shutdown of the fisheries shocked the Island. It forced residents to focus on their collective problems and to look for new ways to make a living. The people of Isle Madame realized that the Island's economy had to be revived by residents themselves—that no one else was going to solve their problems for them. All the community's skill, courage, and intelligence would be required, but people remained hopeful that their lives would be better in the future.

The crisis that hit Isle Madame and so many other Atlantic Canadian communities was summed up in a question many fishermen posed: "No fish in the sea! How can that be?" Though the collapse of the ground fish strategy had meant the loss of 500 jobs, a group of local leaders had anticipated the crisis two years earlier and had come together to find ways to deal with it. They did not engage in denial or fantasies. Instead, they analyzed the problem and suggested remedies. That group included a cross-section of the Island's leadership: trade unionists, educators, small business people, plant workers and managers in the fishing industry, fishermen, youth, seniors, representatives of regional development agencies and municipal councils. Support came from Human Resources Development Canada to set up an Industrial Adjustment Services (IAS) Committee under its programme to aid communities that had lost a major employer.

Recognizing the need for outside expertise, that IAS Committee commissioned GTA Consultants of Halifax to recommend what the community might do in the face of the impending crisis. It got the consultants to involve local residents in the study. Local residents, hired as field workers, held focus-group sessions around the Island, an approach that would make for deeper analysis than would questionnaires and surveys. The focus-group method brings together people with similar backgrounds and expertise to share their reflections and feelings about a common problem. This approach was particularly appropriate on Isle Madame, whose residents had limited reading and writing skills but whose oral traditions were strong. The groups' complex, personal questions required intensive self-examination. From those discussion groups came a number of conclusions. It was obvious that fish stocks were so seriously depleted that it would be some time before they would recover. While many people in the community recognized that hard reality, they were not then thinking realistically about how to deal with it, as statements like these demonstrate: "The government will have to do something," some said. "The plant better look for fish from somewhere else," others warned. People were waiting for someone else to solve the problem.

Idleness and financial pressure made for anxiety in the community. Young people were saddened and discouraged, as they realized that they would not be able to follow their parents' vocations. Most felt they would eventually have to leave Isle Madame and Cape Breton to find work. Participants in the focus groups lacked the confidence and skills to take advantage of government training. "Training for what?" was the question that emerged in all the focus groups. And the prospect of formal training frightened and intimidated many residents.

The GTA Consultants' report, "Charting a New Course," confirmed the seriousness of the situation on Isle Madame, showing that wages and salaries had fallen dramatically over a six year period and that the social fabric of the Island was badly frayed. The community's options were limited—and the situation was unlikely to improve in the near future. The report recommended the creation immediately of a Social Renewal Committee to provide counselling and link displaced fisheries workers with assistance and retraining programmes. It also recommended that an Economic Renewal Committee be set up to create a community economic development strategy. The task at hand was to develop action plans for both committees that could be widely supported by the community, but that would be tied to specific development projects.

In December 1993, Human Resources Development Canada provided funding, through the Community Futures Program, for each committee to hire a full-time officer for seven months. The first task of the Economic Renewal Officer was to solicit residents' and business people's ideas for economic development and job creation. This research generated hundreds of suggestions from 26 community organizations and 140 businesses. The ideas presented were then fed back to those who generated them and to the public at large. The community was asked to rate the potential of each idea. Those ratings formed the basis for a strategic development plan for the Island.

The Social Renewal Task Force contacted every individual directly affected by the downturn in the fisheries. That contact convinced its members that they had to go beyond short-term responses to the immediate crisis. They recognized that they had to consider the long-term prospects of each person in the community as well as the social renewal processes of the community. Deep-rooted attitudes had to be changed, and multifaceted, continuous learning developed if people on Isle Madame who had spent their lives in the fishing industry were to have any future there.

The Economic Renewal and Social Renewal Task Forces made recommendations to the IAS committee. The priorities in their recommendations were boutique tourism, the use of wood products, aquaculture, fishing and seafood production, crafts and small-scale manufacturing, information, entertainment and education, and a "Grey Tiger Strategy," a plan to entice retirees to move to the area. It was suggested that the IAS committee oversee the establishment of a development company to assist existing business, initiate its own ventures, and otherwise improve the Island's business environment. This company would have a full-time human resources officer charged with counselling and providing training programmes that would pay particular attention to life skills, literacy and entrepreneurship. The Human Resources Officer would work closely with the economic renewal team to secure training to prepare people for specific jobs.

The emphasis in all consultations with the community regarding economic and social planning was on reflecting the genuine wishes of the residents of Isle Madame. Only in this way, it was felt, would development plans have a chance of success. Thus did Development Isle Madame (DIMA) emerge as a truly "bottom-up" community initiative.

The recommendations of the IAS committee were submitted to government. Although the report generated much interest, it soon became evident that financial commitment for funding a development company would be difficult to find. Nonetheless, because of the commitment of the IAS committee, several initiatives had already been successfully launched, including TELILE, a Youth Corps Project, and an Aquaculture Extension Office. The IAS committee recommended that DIMA take up where it had left off, and a number of IAS members formed the core of Development Isle Madame. This body came into being in February, 1995. Its mandate was to represent the community and be accountable to it in pursuing the priorities articulated during the IAS process. By the following summer, DIMA had become a community-owned, non-profit limited company. The initial fourteen board members were handpicked to represent all interests in the community. Since its formation, the Board has fluctuated in size from 16 to 22. A number of young people have served on it, as have representatives from the municipal council, Richmond Tourism, and the Strait-Highland Regional Development Agency. Board meetings are open to the public. Working committees tackle specific projects such as the

Small Options Home and the internal financing of it. The Board is still working on establishing a business advisory committee and on developing a call-centre proposal.

Staff members sit on the Board, but not on the Executive. The number of staff depends on the number of projects underway and DIMA's success in securing funding for them. The long-term goal is to become self-sufficient through creating businesses and other opportunities for generating income. Employees serve as planners, start and operate businesses, and provide counselling to local entrepreneurs. The DIMA board held a full-day strategic session for its members and staff to draft a vision statement, identify goals and objectives, and establish project priorities and staff directions. The vision and mission statements have been modified since the creation of DIMA, but the intent has always been to remain true to the original strategic session.

Our vision statement reads:

> We imagine a prosperous Island with a much deeper appreciation of its own strengths: its culture and heritage, its bilingual character, its civility and good humour, its alluring physical environment. It will have a somewhat larger and more diverse population, and a large number of small businesses with solid local roots, commitment to quality and a global perspective.
>
> It will be a community which has a learning culture and in which education for personal satisfaction is as common place as training for a new job or research for a new business venture. A community supportive of its people and its businesses.
>
> In short, it will be very much the Island we already know and love, but with a solid eco-

nomic base and a rich menu of personal and professional options.

And the mission statement summarizes what DIMA is all about:

> Development Isle Madame Limited is dedicated to aid, organize, and foster the necessary social and economic changes on Isle Madame to ensure its future prosperity. Our primary goal is to help in the creation of quality long term sustainable jobs for the residents of Isle Madame.

Much thought went into defining general goals and objectives, and they reflect the way they see the development of the Island:

- To assist in the realization and implementation of the strategic plan of the Island through the integration of development opportunities and educational programs.

- To provide a forum whereby Island residents can contribute to, and take ownership of, the CED process.

- To identify, support, and provide a venue for local community leaders to contribute to the economic development process.

- To assist in the development of infrastructure needed to support economic development.

- To identify and develop small manufacturing opportunities that will maximize the potential of the area and its people.

- To promote Isle Madame as a tourism destination, thereby enriching the environment for service sector growth.

- To assist in building and maintaining a community that will attract youth, former residents, and newcomers to contribute their education and experience to continuing Isle Madame's tradition of being the best place in the world to live.

Community involvement and organizational development helped DIMA secure one-year funding from the Economic Renewal Agency, the Department of Community Services, and the municipality of Richmond. The funds were used to hire a general manager, a development officer and an events co-ordinator. The role of the events co-ordinator is to generate funds at the local level through various activities while raising awareness of the Island's potential to outsiders.

DIMA has been very fortunate in its relationship with Human Resources Development Canada which provided funding for a TAGS (The Atlantic Groundfish Strategy) Liaison Officer. The position was designed to inform local residents about TAGS—to motivate displaced fisheries workers to take training and develop new career plans, and to contact employers for them.

The individual who filled the post really made things happen for DIMA and for many TAGS participants. He had been displaced from the fisheries himself and had volunteered his time and energy to the Island's renewal process. A worker for 20 years at Richmond Fisheries and a representative of the Canadian Auto Workers' Union, he knew everyone engaged in the fishery and had earned their trust and confidence. He was very successful in motivating unemployed individuals to find jobs and explore opportunities. The majority of TAGS clients on Isle Madame have moved toward upgrading, training, and employment. In March 1996, 76 percent of TAGS participants were employed, self-employed, in training or working on local projects. The role of the TAGS Liaison Officer indicates the impact one committed, creative individual can have on a community. DIMA credits him with bringing them a number of projects.

DIMA's strong leadership team has devised new programmes, attracted investment, and inspired community residents. DIMA has gone outside the community for managerial and professional assistance, but has identified skills and resources on the Island, in marketing, finance, computer technology, business management, accounting, public relations and legal services. The community economic development process on Isle Madame relies on the commitment of local people who, though not all professionals, have a genuine interest in developing the community. It has been a long and continuing process of self-education to determine what is needed for local development, to write proposals, seek funds, develop community strategies and motivate people. Each new project brings more and more people into the development process, and their expertise strengthens residents' confidence.

DIMA has undertaken a number of projects in local development in a relatively short time. In its first year of operation, it created six permanent positions and 12 short-term jobs at a Small Options Home. In its second year, DIMA has put most of its efforts into its call-centre initiative, for which funding has been received. Training for positions in the centre has begun, and five permanent jobs were created in the spring of 1997. In three years, this number may double or triple. (Two appendices to this paper present a time line for the revitalization of Isle Madame and the range of activities that have been undertaken already.)

DIMA's development strategies have had to be amended to accommodate forces and factors that emerged as the community animation and mobilization process moved forward. DIMA initially planned its strategy and programmes around efforts to renew the economic life of Isle Madame. Since participation in training programmes and other components of TAGS was not enforced, ways had to be found to encourage and motivate people to start taking personal initiatives to enter training programmes, find alternative employment or start their own ventures. Then, after DIMA spent a great deal of time and energy doing this, the TAGS programme began to emphasize income support rather than training for alternative employment. This has proven very frustrating on Isle Madame, especially as TAGS is scheduled to end in 1998. But DIMA has managed to adapt its development strategies to take advantage of other available programmes, as in 1997, when it used the Employment Insurance Program to provide assistance for individuals and projects.

There have been other frustrations, too. Internal tensions between communities on the Island have caused breakdowns in communication and co-operation. To resolve these problems, DIMA held a series of meetings to establish an Island Council. Informing the community about the crisis and how the Island responds to it has been a challenge from the first day. People understand what job creation means, but they do not have as sure a grasp on the meaning of local development. DIMA has tried a number of tactics to improve community relations; most have been time-consuming and few have been particularly fruitful. In the future, it plans to use newspapers to spread its message and to have media representatives sit in on their board meetings. DIMA has realized that you cannot take for granted that people will get the right message about their efforts at local renewal.

DIMA's creation has strengthened relationships with the municipality, government agencies, and the regional development agency, all of whom are confident of DIMA's ability to achieve its goals. DIMA has also worked with new groups, including Tourism Isle Madame, the Credit Union/DIMA Committee, the Community Investment Fund Committee, and the Isle Madame Committee of Displaced Fishers, to find new ways to inform the community about its work and purpose, and to develop other partnerships. Tourism Isle Madame has focused on signage, marketing and packaging the attractions of the community. The committee formed by the credit union and DIMA discusses the role that a financial institution can play in local development. Business people, local entrepreneurs and DIMA see the possibility of setting up a Community Investment Fund for aquaculture. Local investment should attract other sources of funding, from government and the off-Island financial community. The Isle Madame Committee of Displaced Fishers has worked with DIMA's other organizations, while working in its own way to create a stronger community.

Stable core funding has proven difficult to secure. DIMA's operations are sustained currently by programme funding, some government assistance, and local fund-raising. It has not been an easy task. Government is apparently not prepared to maintain DIMA while it seeks to become self-supporting. Yet DIMA has continued to seek innovative ways to retain staff: funding from a variety of sources enabled it to employ two staff people for most of 1997, and the Board keeps searching for a "cash cow" project to ensure long-term financial stability.

Like many other organizations, DIMA has suffered from volunteers' burnout and has had to develop strategies to cope with it. It has continually recruited new blood with new skills and concern for the community. Unfortunately but not surprisingly, most potential candidates for the DIMA Board are already heavily committed. Advertising for new members and specifying the skills DIMA requires is proving effective in attracting volunteers.

Like many other Cape Breton communities before it, Isle Madame has suffered a brain drain. It has proven difficult to recruit trained professionals with experience in business and community economic development to an agency whose finances are uncertain. Nonetheless, DIMA has been fortunate in stumbling upon well-educated young people seeking experience and committed to the community; the organization has devoted a lot of time to their training and to building up local capacity for a wide range of ventures. Staff are becoming more competent with each task they undertake. The TAGS Liaison Officer has also grown with the job.

In a short time, DIMA has found technical assistance in a wide range of agencies and have become partners with them, agencies like Human Resources Development Canada, Enterprise Cape Breton Corporation, the Economic Renewal Agency (now the Department of Economic Development and Tourism), the provincial Departments of Education and Culture, Fisheries and Natural Resources, Heritage Canada, local credit unions, parish priests, community college and high school, the business community and many community organizations. And DIMA is also affiliated with the Coastal Communities Network and the University College of Cape Breton, through its Community Economic Development (CED) Institute.

DIMA's development strategy has never been definitively articulated. It has been hard to develop strategy when change has been so rapid and the variables so numerous. Many times, DIMA has had to shift position in midstream, as situations continued to change. Only by continually re-evaluating its priorities, projects, and capabilities has DIMA been able to make progress. The Board feels that now our development strategy can be completed.

DIMA achieved what it has because community leaders anticipated the fisheries crisis and began to plan for it before the closure of the ground fishery. They have succeeded because of the network of contacts and partnerships locally and beyond the Island that enables them to get what they need, when they need it. What is more, Isle Madame has dynamic, concerned and committed residents willing to look beyond personal and local issues and work for the benefit of the whole community. The crisis has brought the people of the Island together and they have learned how to handle the tensions and pressures that change makes inevitable.

Isle Madame is still a community in transition, from a stable past based on a traditional industry to an uncertain future. After two years, DIMA can begin to appreciate its successes and failures. Its members no longer feel they are working in a void. Organizing themselves has been a long and difficult process, but a powerful alliance among all sectors of the community has emerged. Despite its limitations, DIMA has brought hope to what looked like a hopeless situation. Increasingly, it has become Isle Madame's facilitator and animator, leading the community and encouraging its members to solve individual and collective problems through focused and informed action.

APPENDIX 1:
TIME LINE

1990 - 91:

Fishery down-turn

1992:

Isle Madame Industrial Adjustment Service Committee (IAS) formed

1993:

GTA Consultant Report "Isle Madame - Charting a New Course"

1994:

Isle Madame IAS Committee response to GTA report:

Economic Renewal Task Force/Social Renewal Task Force

IAS Report and recommendations

Telile (community television station created)

Youth Corps Project

1995:

Development Isle Madame created—a strategic management session held

TAGS Liaison Officer hired

Richmond County Aquaculture Extension Office opened

Isle Madame Small Option Home opened

Isle Madame World Wide Web site created

Isle Madame Heritage Regions

Volunteer Isle Madame - Senior Care

1996:

Richmond County Coastal Mapping Project

Grey Tigers article (attracting early retirees to Isle Madame)

Isle Madame information package created

Call Centre research underway

Home-Based sewing project

Cod Stock '96

Tourism Isle Madame formed

Production Picasse

AFL Oil Tank Manufacturing project

1997:

TradeWinds Call Centre Incorporated

Cap Auguet Trail project

Aquaculture project

Community Investment Fund

APPENDIX 2:
ACTIVITIES

Development Isle Madame Projects (in some cases, projects were partnered with other organizations)

Informing The Public

Good News Expo

Community News Letter

Community Economic Development Awareness Project

Board Meetings Open to the Public

Press Releases

Infrastructure (Promotion and Knowledge Base)

Tourism Operator Seminar - resulting in Tourism Isle Madame

Isle Madame Tourism Brochure

Cape Auget EcoTrail

Aquaculture Extension Office

Community Investment Fund

Isle Madame World Wide Web Site

Richmond County Coastal Zone Mapping Project

Grey Tigers - Canadian Yachting Article

Isle Madame Information Package

Isle Madame Community Resiliency Roadside Beautification (tree planting, fire hydrants)

Marine Tough Tank

CED Partnership Committee Between DIMA and St. Joseph Credit Union

Internal Financing

Movies

Isle Madame Logo Retail Items

Cod Stock '96

Special Events

Project Administration Fee - Business Proposals

Revenue Generating Business Projects - Long Term Goal

Job Creation/Training

Isle Madame Small Options Home

Isle Madame Commercial Centre

Home Based Sewing Project

Greg's Fuels Tank Manufacturing

Production Picasse

Tire Recycling Plant

Isle Madame Call Centre

Renewed Fishery Proposals

Aquaculture Development

ENTERPRISE CAPE BRETON CORPORATION: WHERE TOP DOWN MEETS BOTTOM UP

KEITH G. BROWN

THE CED CONTEXT

To many, coupling a federal crown corporation with CED is an oxymoron. Indeed, debate continues about what CED means, but I would argue that for most of its history, ECBC has been an instrument of community development.

Throughout most of its history, the Corporation has been guided by its community and has provided support in myriad ways to local development organizations, community groups and individuals, all seeking economic diversification. Some successes have been stellar, some failures dismal. Some never worked; some are still faltering in the present and will ultimately fail. But when local vision, entrepreneurial spirit, market forces and corporate investment have come together, spectacular, made-in-Cape Breton achievements have resulted.

In some regions of Canada, the perception is that Cape Breton Island has received federal transfer payments since Confederation. The facts tell a different story. At the turn of the last century, Sydney, a small sleepy town on Sydney

Harbour, was the scene of rapid and dramatic industrialization. Thousands of immigrants from Eastern Europe and the Caribbean flocked to the region to work in steel. The coal industry was expanding and it too attracted thousands of European settlers. The largest industrial complex in Atlantic Canada took shape in Cape Breton County. During World War II, Sydney Harbour was second only to Halifax in the Canadian convoy deployment that supplied Europe with its lifeline. Indeed, for the first half of the 20th century, Cape Breton was the heavy industrial giant of the Atlantic Provinces. This industrialization was spawned by a few large international firms, some of which built entire towns in Cape Breton. Thousands occupied company houses, shopped at company stores, lived their lives in company communities. Dependence upon the "company" fostered a notion that "they" were responsible to provide for Cape Bretoners. Then, as "they" lost interest in Cape Breton, Cape Bretoners turned to government; one "they" replaced another. No cultural attitudinal shift occurred; we had worked for companies we didn't own and now, Big Brother would provide. By and large, Cape Bretoners were merely bystanders in their own economy. The profitability of coal and steel continued to drop. By the 1960s, the situation had reached crisis proportions. Then, the government stepped in.

This chapter explores the decision of the Government of Canada to create a crown corporation to address the coal crisis on Cape Breton. It examines the principal strategic directions of the Corporation from 1967 to 1997, and highlights its success in building a tourism industry on the Island and its lesser successes in aquaculture. When it has been successful, it has done so as the result of broad and diversified public input, reshaping itself to meet the changing needs of its community.

Community Economic Development (CED) is a broad arena that brings many participants together for a common good. Here is the OECD's definition of CED:

Local economic development is a general but diverse social process whereby actors and institutions mobilize to take initiatives to transform the local economy and create new activities, businesses and jobs, or consolidate existing ones by exploiting and enhancing local resources and local potential. These often scattered and spontaneous initiatives trigger off a process of sustainable development; inasmuch as they are part of coherent local approaches, they lead to the emergence of innovative mechanisms and new patterns of organization, they foster new projects, and help to cultivate entrepreneurship, and, finally they bring together and involve all partners in the local economy.[1]

Dr. Michael Porter of the Harvard Business School has written widely on competitive advantage, most recently in *The Competitive Advantage of Nations*. On the issue of regional economic development policies, he writes that:

Regional economic development policies, another popular government initiative, are also often misguided. Many nations and states attempt to lure industries to remote areas or to regions that are economically depressed. Large subsidies, for example, have persuaded steel and auto companies to build greenfield sites in such areas of Italy and the United Kingdom. The result is usually disastrous. The investments fail because they are not connected to a critical mass of suppliers or research institutions. A better approach to regional policy employs the concept of clustering, building on already existing or nascent areas of strength and attempting to expand and upgrade them.[2]

There is no dichotomy in these statements; in fact, the two positions can be analogous. While Dr. Porter builds his case for the development of an industrial/knowledge base that is internationally competitive and global in nature, he locates that base in the local community. Granted, by local he often seems to mean national; nonetheless, he presents cases of international competitiveness rooted firmly in localized renewable activities:

> Home-based competitors in related industries with similar skills, technologies, or customers, provide similar benefits: information flow, technical interchange, and opportunities for sharing that increase the rate of innovation and upgrading...The process of innovating and upgrading is inherently local. A company's home base...where its strategy for global competition is set and where its research on products and processes is carried out—is vital to its competitive advantage. To explain the role of the home base is to answer the key question about international competitiveness today: what are the attributes of a nation, state or city that foster the ability of its companies to innovate and upgrade in a particular industry?[3]

Let's explore this thesis more closely. One of the leading minds on global economic development strategies tells us, in essence: do what you do well, refine it, do it better and export to the world. And remember that global competitiveness is inherently local.

The OECD definition talks of innovative mechanisms and Dr. Porter speaks of cluster innovation. Can we apply these two concepts to Cape Breton? CED is based upon local ownership and control; maximum use of local resources; enterprise activities that create new businesses; linkages of education, enterprise development and employment creation and healthy working environments. Dr. Porter argues that we must do CED within a global context. We turn to a case.

Several sectors demonstrate the Corporation's focus on CED. We will examine two of its more significant investments.

TOURISM

Before the birth of the Corporation, Cape Breton's Cabot Trail attracted motoring tourists. Fixed-roof accommodation was limited to small motels and some small tourist lodges in Sydney, Cheticamp, Baddeck and Ingonish. The Keltic Lodge in Ingonish catered to the upscale market. Attractions were limited. The season spanned part of July and August. From its earliest years, the Corporation recognized the tremendous potential of tourism as a generator of income and employment and began supporting local tourist associations. While the private investors recognized the potential of tourism, few were willing to risk substantial investment. The Corporation moved in to fill this void, its focus areas being those that had great physical beauty but little employment outside of fishing and forestry. Over a decade, the Corporation embarked upon an ambitious programme to develop fixed-roof accommodation, food and beverage attractions and marketing programmes. As tourism expanded, the Corporation helped the private sector through its loan programmes to establish Bed-and-Breakfast facilities and to upgrade other kinds of accommodations. In many areas, tourism began to be seen as a principal employer, rather than as a marginal, six- to eight-week augmentation of family income. More than a decade after the first tourism operations were established by IDD, they were generating in excess of $1 million revenue for the Corporation. (IDD, the Industrial Development Division of the Cape Breton Development Corporation, a precursor to ECBC, is discussed later in this chapter.) As the private sector strengthened, the Corporation began to divest itself of its tourism operations. Most of these facilities continue to operate today as private companies, employing hundreds of people in rural Cape Breton for a season that now extends from May until October.

The tourism community then turned to the Corporation for other services and expertise, particularly to develop a well-researched, concerted plan for marketing the entire Island as a tourist destination. Historically, areas of the Island saw each other as competitors. IDD/ECBC helped change that. With input from tourist operators on Cape Breton, IDD/ECBC developed international award-winning advertising campaigns for the whole Island, and began to do co-operative advertising with the Province of Nova Scotia as well. Today, IDD/ECBC even dedicates a portion of its marketing budget to be administered by Tourism Cape Breton, the local tourism association. The journey had begun with ECBC's recognition that an industry could be developed. The industry has become vastly more sophisticated than in the early 1970s when IDD was the largest tourist operator on Cape Breton. Expanded private facilities and international marketing have made tourism one of the most important employers on Cape Breton: 5,500 people today tie their incomes to the $180 million generated in 1997.

Aquaculture

Not all initiatives of the Corporation were as successful as its tourism experience. As early as the 1970s, some foresaw that the Bras d'Or Lakes and the coastal waters surrounding Cape Breton might support aquaculture. The notion was new to Atlantic Canada in the early 1970s, at least as an alternative to traditional offshore fishing. The Corporation responded by investing in Cape Breton Marine Farming Ltd. The company would do research and development, grow stock, harvest, process and market; in the terminology of the nineties, it would be a fully integrated company. As the aquaculture programme grew, it began to consume an ever-larger portion of the Corporation's operating budget. There also began to be cries to privatize. The company was spun off to form several smaller companies, owned by former corporate employees, in an attempt to do what the OECD definition calls "cultivating entrepreneurship." At the same time, aquacultural development began to falter throughout Nova Scotia. A decade ago, the production from this sector was roughly equal in Nova Scotia and New Brunswick. New Brunswick invested heavily in research facilities, specializing and actively encouraging entry into the industry. Nova Scotia did not follow suit. Within ten years, New Brunswick's production in this industry outstripped Nova Scotia, exceeding it now by 1000 percent. Cape Breton represents more than 40 percent of Nova Scotia's output. In Cape Breton, the industry has been plagued with production problems and disease. Few operators have been able to make the transition to high volume, profitable businesses, yet operators still want to expand their facilities and experiment with new species.

The Corporation's performance in aquaculture is much debated. Many accountants argue that ECBC has thrown good money after bad; some former Marine Farming employees, still operating their own businesses, suggest that ECBC was ahead of its time and that success is just around the corner. Critics of IDD/ECBC (and there have been many over the years) charge that the Corporation tried to be all things to all people on Cape Breton. Yet the politicians who created the Corporation recognized that for many thousands of Cape Bretoners, the Corporation was their last hope. Indeed, ECBC was involved with hundreds of failed ventures over 30 years, but it was involved too with many thousands of successes. In success as in failure, the Corporation "…involved all partners in the local community." As the needs of the community changed, so too did the Corporation's response. The failed tourism operator may look upon the ECBC's 30 years of tourism development as holding out false hope. But the successful aquaculture entrepreneur may see the corporate investment as an investment in his future. That has long been the dilemma of IDD/ECBC: success is very much in the eye of the beholder. Through success and failure, the Corporation was involved in virtually every community on Cape Breton Island and later in Mulgrave, on the mainland of Nova Scotia, working with their visions and dreams.

How does a development corporation inculcate entrepreneurism in a culture that has historically looked to others for the solutions? One approach has been to have local Cape Bretoners work for the Corporation. Throughout the years, the sons and daughters of miners, steelworkers, fishers and foresters have worked as staff with local people. While they had to operate within bureaucratic systems, staff attempted to design local programmes for local needs. Much rode on the success of this approach. Staff members lived in the coal towns and small rural communities; their children were schooled there and they too were trying to secure a better standard of living for their families and friends. Staff could not look to Ottawa for solutions; their job was to help Cape Bretoners find their own solutions.

Enterprise Cape Breton Corporation (ECBC), a federal Crown Corporation born of the Industrial Development Division (IDD) of the Cape Breton Development Corporation, has arguably the broadest mandate for economic development in Canada. The legislative capacity of the Corporation came from a recognition that Cape Breton's cornerstones, coal and steel, were in danger of complete collapse. The Prime Minister of the day, The Right Honourable Lester B. Pearson, deemed the economic crisis in Cape Breton to be "in the national interest." He instructed his government to help diversify the economy of Cape Breton Island beyond coal mining, and to prepare for the orderly closure of the mines.

IDD/ECBC has, in its 30 years, survived restructuring, marginalization, merger and attempts at closure. It has always been an anomaly in the federal system, in that its authority is delegated to a local Board of Directors. For most of its life, it has not been integrated within the federal bureaucracy, though there have been attempts to bring it in line with government departments with similar objectives.

With its corporate mandate legislatively restricted to Cape Breton Island and Mulgrave, IDD/ECBC had to stay flexible, responding at times in ways not necessarily reflective of national economic policy.

THE CAPE BRETON COAL PROBLEM

The economy of Cape Breton County has long been fuelled by coal. Cape Breton mining and its downstream sister industry of steel represented the largest concentration of heavy industry in Atlantic Canada:

> These two industries with 10,500 employees, employed more than one-third of the wage earners in Cape Breton County in 1965. To place the problem in perspective in relation to Nova Scotia as a whole, at the time of the 1961 Census, the population of Cape Breton County represented 14 per cent of the total provincial population.[4]

The Dominion Steel and Coal Company (DOSCO) was operating No. 12 (most mines were denoted by colliery number) in New Waterford, No. 18 in New Victoria, No. 20 and No. 26 in Glace Bay and Princess in Sydney Mines. In 1960, the Royal Commission on Coal recommended that the subsidization of the Sydney fields be curtailed. But the Government of Canada continued to subsidize coal operations to lessen the provincial reliance upon imported offshore oil.

The Cape Breton Coal Problem report recommended that the Governments of Canada and Nova Scotia form a crown corporation to lessen the impact of mine closures and broaden the base of the Island's economy:

> As a result of geographic location and low-cost water transport, Cape Breton can draw upon world-wide sources of materials. With imaginative market exploration, intelligent planning and adequate financing, opportunities can undoubtedly be found and projects developed which will strengthen the economy and provide diversified employment.[5]

The Right Honourable Lester B. Pearson, in his December 1966 policy statement on Cape Breton coal said that:

> The federal government realizes that the Cape Breton coal problem is essentially a social one. It is because of its awareness of, and concern for, the well-being of individuals and their communities that the federal government is prepared to assist, on a massive scale, the transition of the areas from dependence on a declining natural resource to a sound economic base...The Government of Canada and the Government of Nova Scotia believe that a rigid adherence to a fixed time-table to reduce the level of coal production might involve unnecessary hardship on the dependent communities. Consequently, the rationalization of the mines will be related to the success in the introduction of new industries. The Crown Corporation will be instructed to give full consideration to the needs of orderly adjustment, including the implementation of a generous early retirement plan for the miners as recommended by Dr. Donald.[6]

Following Parliamentary review and approval, the Cape Breton Development Corporation Act was given Royal Assent on July 7, 1967 and in accordance with Section 36, came into force on October 1, 1967. At that time, the Corporation recorded a staff complement of 6,278.

The legislation made provision for two divisions in the Corporation, coal and industrial development. The remainder of this chapter will deal with the Industrial Development Division (IDD) and its successor, Enterprise Cape Breton Corporation (ECBC).

INDUSTRIAL DEVELOPMENT DIVISION

The Government of Canada gave birth to an organization that, arguably, had the broadest mandate for economic development in the country. The only stipulation in the act limiting the powers of IDD is that it must "provide employment outside the coal producing industry." Its objects and powers meant that IDD had the ability to make loans or grants to individuals or organizations, take equity positions in private companies or to establish, own and operate operations or wholly owned subsidiary companies of the Corporation. The Government of Canada's original investment in IDD was $20 million; the Government of Nova Scotia's was $10 million.

1967-1972

In its earliest annual reports, the Corporation reported difficulty recruiting "adequately trained personnel" who would agree to relocate to Cape Breton. One of the drawbacks for those it recruited was lack of apartment and office space and meeting facilities. Manufacturing was the first focus for diversification, Cape Breton's natural resources and location on tidewater being prime assets to that industry.

Thus, the earliest objective was providing industrial infrastructure in projects like financing for the Gulf Oil Refinery wharf in Point Tupper, acquisition of the former naval base in Point Edward for conversion to an industrial park (later to be called Sydport), large-scale reforestation at Cape Smokey and a loan guarantee for Nova Scotia Forestry Industries (now Stora) in Port Hawkesbury. And to provide accommodations for personnel and others, the Corporation, through its wholly owned subsidiary company, DARR Cape Breton Ltd., constructed Cabot House, an 18-storey apartment and office complex, and adjacent to it, the Holiday Inn in Sydney.

Because of their potential for job creation, tourism and recreation were added to the Corporation's priority list, and the first efforts to market the Island as a tourism destination began. It was in this period that the Corporation became a tourism operator, as it constructed or purchased amenities or attractions. The Corporation also explored resource development, particularly oyster culture and other marine farming and sheep were imported to increase the flock on the Island.

As the initial five-year segment ended, the Corporation recognized that grassroots development should be encouraged and that "footloose" industries should not be enticed to relocate to Cape Breton. The danger that such industries would appear was real, especially given the inability to attract manufacturing industry to Cape Breton in those first years.

1973-1978

This era was one of rapid expansion of corporate-owned facilities, as the Corporation moved to expand infrastructure. Thus it was during this era that most of the facilities the Corporation would long be identified with were constructed: Dundee Resort, Inverness Beach Village, Whale Cove Cottages, the buildings at the Miners' Village, the four Chowder Houses, the period restaurants and bakery at the Fortress of Louisbourg, Louisbourg Reproductions, and the expansion of Island Crafts. Aquaculture research also grew to include soft shell clams, trout, Pacific and Atlantic salmon and the cultivation of seaweeds.

Support for community groups or sectoral federations began in earnest with corporate investment in the Christmas Tree Association, the Beekeepers Association, and the Information and Archival Centre in Cheticamp. During the same time, IDD instituted its first loan programmes for upgrading hotel/motel/tourist homes to expand its investments into the private sector.

1979-1984

During this phase, the Corporation's investments moved away from tourism facilities and into industrial infrastructure, with substantial upgrades at Sydport and the construction of incubator industry centres in Louisdale, Inverness and Sydport. Agriculture and forestry also benefited from corporate acquisition of lands in Mabou and Point Edward for demonstration farms that would investigate new practices for increasing production and farm gate sales.

Announcements of oil and gas finds in the Sable Fields and offshore Newfoundland heightened interest in the Ports of Sydney and Strait of Canso as supply and manufacturing centres to service expected offshore activities. IDD became very involved in marketing the Island for gas- and oil-related activities.

As the economy began to diversify, the number of small private firms who received direct assistance grew. Craft production rose dramatically: individual producers were offered direct and marketing assistance, and the wholesale and retail activities of Island Crafts were supported. Bed-and-Breakfast programmes, providing loan assistance for the upgrade of individual homes for tourist use, were implemented.

To provide career-related summer employment for Cape Breton youth in conjunction with providing much needed expertise to local firms, IDD developed and implemented its Career Enrichment Program.

1985-1990

There is little doubt that these years were some of the most tumultuous for the Corporation, as its focus shifted dramatically away from owner/operator to animator for strategic sectoral research and investment. In 1985, the Corporation undertook the largest review of its programming since 1967, a review that sought wide-scale public input.

In the 1984/85 Annual Report, the Corporation says that:

> The 1984/85 fiscal year was one of reassessment of the Industrial Development Division's operating policies and objectives. A thorough review was conducted of all existing programs and investments. All facets of the Corporation's own companies were examined as well.
>
> In conjunction with the internal review, the Division conducted a public debate, using the forum of open meetings, to obtain input into the programs deemed necessary by the private sector to stimulate economic growth.[7]

The review and the public input sessions dramatically changed the course of the IDD for the rest of the decade. To encourage private sector investment, the Corporation sold its interests in Inverness Beach Village, C.B. Woollen Mills Ltd., Cape Breton Marine Farming Ltd., Dundee Resort, Island Crafts, and the restaurants at the Fortress of Louisbourg.

The Government of Canada commissioned an analysis of the Cape Breton economy through the Cape Breton Advisory

Committee Report. That committee, chaired by Dr. Teresa McNeil, recommended the creation of a stand-alone crown corporation for economic development on Cape Breton. Accordingly in December 1985, the government created Enterprise Cape Breton as a federal agency, not a federal Crown Corporation. ECBC was empowered to develop five-year programmes specific to Cape Breton Island. Enterprise Cape Breton, not to be confused with Enterprise Cape Breton Corporation, was to promote one-stop business and industry shopping for assistance, with local authority on Cape Breton. ECB became part of the Atlantic Canada Opportunities Agency (ACOA), which had inherited the mandate and programmes of DRIE (the Department of Regional Industrial Expansion). ECB represented ACOA on Cape Breton.

The Government of Canada announced its decision to amend the Cape Breton Development Corporation Act in 1988, so as to remove the Industrial Development Division and its activities from the Corporation and replace the IDD with a stand-alone Crown Corporation, to be called Enterprise Cape Breton Corporation (ECBC). Cape Bretoners were concerned. Newspaper editors, individuals and organizations in the hundreds expressed their concern that the soul of IDD, and its connection to the community, was being severed. The Cape Breton Development Corporation prepared its response to the Government of Canada. In it, the President and Chairperson of the Board, Dr. Teresa McNeil, argued that:

> The statutory mandate, financial authorities and operational experience of the Industrial Development Division of DEVCO have allowed it to develop a flexible, wide-ranging and down-to-earth approach to economic development, one that has given it strong credibility among the entrepreneurs and workers of the Island. In any new configuration of the governmental institutions concerned with eco-

nomic development, the principal elements of this approach should be retained and strengthened. Single-program replacements will not satisfy the obvious need for continuation of a comprehensive set of industrial support services similar to those provided by the IDD.[8]

Public and private debate continued. The principal issue was not legislative authority since Bill C-103, the bill which would create ECBC, deemed ECBC essentially to be a continuation of IDD, having all of IDD's objects and powers. In effect, legally ECBC would be treated as if it had been in existence since 1967, and would be held responsible for the past commitments of IDD.

It was the far more ethereal issue of the soul of IDD, and its intrinsic commitment to community-based economic development, that caused outcry. Two Parliamentary Committee hearings were conducted on Bill C-103, one in Port Hawkesbury and one in Ottawa. On the topic of social conscience, Senator Cochran posed the question to the Vice-President, Keith G. Brown. Brown replied:

> The social conscience is not an instrument of legislation. It is an instrument of policy of a board of directors, and that is very clear. This ECBC will have whatever social conscience its board of directors decides it shall have, and that is how the social conscience of the Cape Breton Development Corporation has evolved. It is a 20 year conscience within a framework of legislation that permits it to have a conscience.[9]

On December 1, 1988, legislation was enacted to create an autonomous federal crown corporation for Cape Breton Island and Mulgrave which would diversify the economy of the geographic area beyond coal mining. The addition of

Mulgrave to the mandate corrected a long-standing problem that precluded corporate assistance on the western side of the Strait of Canso.

1991-1996

In November 1990, Elmer MacKay, Minister Responsible for the Atlantic Canada Opportunities Agency, which had assumed responsibility for ECB, announced an independent assessment of that Agency's operations. Gardner Pinfold of Halifax provided macroeconomic analysis, Deloitte and Touche of Halifax analyzed projects and overall programmes, Seaconsult of St. John's prepared reports from computerized data, and Coastal Associates of St. John's co-ordinated the various assessments. A.A. Brait chaired the review. Mr. Brait recommended streamlining and clarifying the federal presence in economic development assistance in Cape Breton. The government responded by announcing that ECB, which had a five-year sunset clause, would be permitted to cease operations in March of 1991.

ECBC would be the chief federal presence on the Island, delivering its programmes in conjunction with ACOA. While there was no legislative need to do so, ECBC chose to closely mirror the operating practices of its sister agency ACOA, which, for many Cape Bretoners, cost it its former distinctiveness. In 1992, the Government of Canada announced, in Bill C-93, that federal funding to dozens of organizations and institutions, including ECBC, would be curtailed. On June 3, 1993, Senator B. Alaistair Graham spoke against the bill. Perhaps better than most, as the original Secretary to the Cape Breton Development Corporation, Senator Graham understood the processes, the nuance and confusion in the minds of the public around IDD, ECBC, ECB and ACOA:

> ...Enterprise Cape Breton, ECB, as distinct from ECBC was already in place. Originally

> ECB was to be a unique regional development agency to complement the Industrial Development Division of Devco. ECB turned out to be just the Cape Breton branch office of ACOA. But ECBC was allegedly created to carry on the mandate of the Industrial Development Division of Devco...Sounds confusing? It was. It is. And I believe it was intended to be confusing.[10]

Bill C-93 was defeated in the Senate, and the government of the day dissolved before the Bill could be reintroduced. ECBC had a new lease on life. In the Spring of 1994, however, the Government of Canada announced that the ACOA Cape Breton office would close and that ACOA's programmes thereafter would be administered and delivered by ECBC. The Corporation had gone full circle: the proactive initiator of the 1970s and early 1980s had become somewhat of a bystander as, in the mid-1980s, ECB was born. In the early 1990s, its role was confused when the Corporation became more closely integrated with ACOA. In 1994, it emerged, phoenix-like, to be the singular federal presence in economic development on Cape Breton Island.

Here are 30 years in perspective: the cornerstone of the Cape Breton economy had collapsed and the Government of Canada looked to diversify that economy. The Crown Corporation empowered to do so had a broad mandate. For most of its history, ECBC has responded to the changing needs of Cape Breton through dramatically different strategies and approaches to economic development. However, the common thread in all the Corporation's work has been the commitment to the community.

So where are we today? Have the OECD's definition of CED and Dr. Porter's theories on local innovation taken hold in Cape Breton? Three decades later, has the goal of diversifying the economy of Cape Breton taken hold? Have we accepted that our future is in diversification, and in home-grown answers and new technologies? Though coal and steel remain important in the economy, they are mere shadows of their former selves; where more than 10,000 worked, now less than 3,000 do. Porter's "clusters" are developing on the Island and ECBC is following its constituents' direction.

For example, academic interest, technological know-how, a culture rich with music and storytelling and the entrepreneurial spirit have come together to produce unique multimedia experiments. Let's put this in context: a multibillion dollar global industry, at home in Orlando and Los Angeles with the Spielbergs and Disneys, can take root and flourish in Cape Breton. Not long ago, surely this would be seen as folly or hallucinogenic government policy. These few local firms were, in large part, virtually undercapitalized, lacked marketing expertise, and were located on the periphery of the continent. But a 21st-century CED vehicle, the Technology Advisory Group, came together to share information and transfer knowledge and technology to Cape Breton. More and more people began to showcase their interest and talents in this rapidly growing world industry of "edutainment." Research and debate and travel to trade shows fuelled further debate and as the process continued, a "cluster" (in Porter's terminology) began to take shape. The initial apprehension of being too small to effectively compete with the major players, too small to be taken seriously in the boardrooms of Houston or New York, gave way to the germ of an idea of coming together to share resources while remaining independent and autonomous. "Silicon Island" was born. Local businesses would turn a formerly sick municipal building near a park into a state-of-the-art multimedia cluster and market Cape Breton's ingenuity to the rest of the world. Government was asked to provide the infrastructure, a role that Porter argues is one of the key roles of government in economic development. In 1998, Silicon Island will open its doors and ports to the world—minutes from the Atlantic Ocean and seconds from Tokyo, London and New York. Digital animation, virtual reality, interactive distance education, media production, CD-ROM development—all will be sent down the fibre cable to the world. A local idea can take on the world. A made-in-Cape Breton contribution will help to further diversify the local economy. This, I would argue, is global CED, Cape Breton style.

Is Silicon Island an anomaly in this Island, where we once worked for the company but never owned it, where we extracted natural resources unmindful of ecological cost, and where we looked for solutions from "away"? Simply put, no!

Ten years ago, before the celebrated success of Rita McNeil and the Rankins, before the Barra MacNeils, Ashley MacIsaac and Natalie MacMaster, a group of local entertainers and would-be promoters argued successfully to the Cape Breton Development Corporation that entertainment could be an industry on Cape Breton—for vocalists and musicians, but also for recording technicians, lighting crews and technical staff. Many wondered where, with Nashville and Toronto and Los Angeles supplying American music to the world, would be the niche for home-grown talent. The key here is the niche. Making music in church halls and firehalls and playing for $20 is fun, but it is not an industry. The mass market is not interested in traditional Celtic music, so what does one do? Groups came together and talked. Community groups wanting to celebrate their local festivals came on side. Artists took traditional music and gave it a distinctive upbeat Cape Breton style. Or they dug deep for the old, haunting tales from a time when there was nothing but community and neighbourly support, reminding urban Canada of a simpler, harsher life. The new sound was marketed and showcased, the promoters were brought here to see and hear for themselves and the community performed. The sound sold in

Canada and the United Kingdom, and five million disks later, Rita MacNeil and the Rankins are major promoters of the Cape Breton sound. Local technicians wanted to keep the technical side of music-making on the Island, and indeed, Cape Breton recording studios are now charting the course for performers from here and from Toronto and Ireland, as well. Once more, as with multimedia, we are not only *not* on the periphery; we are at the very centre of the cultural industries in Canada. This, too, involves home-grown commitment and dedication done within a wider context—of lawyers in New York, accountants in Toronto and technicians in Point Aconi, Cape Breton. Millions of dollars of new income and hundreds of jobs come from a renewable resource of endless talent. Once again, a Cape Breton solution is wrapped within a Porter cluster.

Is there a contradiction to CED and globalization? I would put forward the thesis that the two are inextricably linked. We who are practitioners or academics in CED must encourage local communities and community groups to embrace globalization and its opportunities to supply innovative, entrepreneurial goods and services for regional, national and international demands.

As ECBC charts its course for the new millennium, it seeks direction from the community at large. In doing so, it respects the soul of an organization and humanizes the bureaucratic process. There is much improvement to be done. ECBC will do so with its community.

ENDNOTES

1. Personal correspondence, OECD, Paris, 1994.
2. Michael E. Porter, PhD, *The Competitive Advantage of Nations*. Boston: Harvard College, 1993, p. 8.
3. Ibid. p. 6.
4. J.R. Donald, *The Cape Breton Coal Problem* Montreal: 1966, p. 4.

5. Ibid. p. 24.

6. The Right Honourable Lester Pearson, Ottawa, 1966, p. 1.

7. Cape Breton Development Corporation, *Annual Report*, Sydney, N.S., 1985, p. 7.

8. Cape Breton Development Corporation, a paper prepared for purposes of discussion. Sydney, N.S., 1987, p. 14.

9. Government of Canada, Legislative Committee on Bill C-103, *Minutes of Proceedings and Evidence*, Port Hawkesbury, N.S. 3:44.

10. Government of Canada, Senate, *Debates* on Bill C-93, June 3, 1993, p. 3376.

Part 3

Technology and Community Economic Development

9

INFORMATION AND COMMUNICATIONS TECHNOLOGY AND LOCAL ECONOMIC DEVELOPMENT
MICHAEL GURSTEIN

Once a generation, an issue or event becomes a defining experience. Earlier in this century, it was the Great Depression. For this generation, straddling two centuries, the issue that will give this era its definition will be, almost certainly, globalization. In the economic sphere, globalization is not simply opening-up of new production networks or penetrating overseas markets. It is a complete reshaping of the nature and organization of business, along with an overwhelming rush to restructure and adjust the supporting political and legal frameworks.

This evolution of the global economy and the forced restructuring of national, regional and local economies that it forces can be traced, in part, to the widespread availability of low-cost Information and Communications Technologies (ICTs). Instantaneous communication of purchase orders, cash transfers, remote commands to production robots and the daily flow of millions of electronic mail messages, permits management at a distance and the accumulation and agglomeration of power at the hubs of the globalized economy.

Globalization, however, is only the most recent manifestation of the ongoing trend toward metropolitan centralization. The emergence of global concentrations of wealth and power follows the well-worn path of the persistent asymmetrical power relations between the metropolitan area and the periphery. Wealth, power, skills and innovation are concentrated at the centre; economic well-being disappears in the peripheral regions. But the metropolitan centre is no longer necessarily a strictly physical location—a city or region. Rather, there is the new "virtual" metropolis, which may or may not have a physical manifestation. This centre of power and control resides primarily in the communications network that links those who make decisions with those who they control, as production workers or consumers.

The global model, which is being realized at an astonishing pace, is a system of seamless, frictionless technology enabling production and distribution, placement and displacement. The notion of frictionless flows of capital, goods, and people through electronic marketplaces is intriguing, especially for those who would end up as the winners.[1] Frictionless capitalism is presented as a way to enhance efficiency and respond to consumer choice. But in reality, it brings local producers in ever-wider swaths of economic activity and local producers into fearsome competition for investment with globally-distributed corporations. With capital and production perceived as infinitely mobile (frictionless), and always seeking the highest return, the competition is never-ending and is all-pervasive in productive life.

In real life, the globalized economy will have few winners and very many losers, and the winners are very big winners indeed. But there can be only so many winners. What happens to everyone else in the globalized, frictionless, virtual world of the future?[2]

Many in the real world now are attempting to use the technology to create a world where many can participate *as* and *where* they are; indeed, the new technology can provide powerful tools to do so. The key, however, in the real world is not living in a virtual city. It involves living in a real, fixed (even anchored) location in place and time, where technology is not a release from a burden of place but rather, a response to the challenge and opportunities of the locale.

It is useful to look at local economic development as a form of resistance—to globalization, to the need to emigrate to find meaningful and reasonably paid work, to the inevitability of metropolitanization and of globalization. Using notions of place, loyalty, community and family as criteria for economic decision-making runs counter to the prevailing emphasis on globalized return for globalized investment. It may seem odd to talk of resistance as a form of economic development. But by refusing to accept prevailing norms for local investment/local development, this is precisely what its proponents are attempting.

Developing a local enterprise with local linkages and local responsibilities is, in fact, an act of resistance. Small entrepreneurs who overcome the costs and penalties of being locally enterprising are no less heroic than those who try to sustain local communities in the face of centralization, the cutting-back of social safety nets and deregulation of transportation and utility tariffs.

Economic globalization hollows out local communities. More knowledge-intensive activities are centralized. An artificial specialization is forced onto the local economy. Local production is put into a global wage and benefit, tax and utility-offset competition. The results include local decline because financial and public services are centralized, and because of the arrival of big-box retailers, and because processing and production become increasingly sophisticated technologically. Thus, local communities become ever more subject to external forces over which they have little or no control. As the globalized economy becomes more technologically sophisticated, the need for capital increases. Meanwhile, capital available for local investment declines and the pressure to invest for short-term returns increases. The life or death of local economies becomes simply a by-product of what many are terming the *Casino Economy*. Local investment, local production, jobs and economic activity become subject to decisions made in volatile financial markets, greatly removed from local impacts and accountability.

Globalization of even the most remote and small-scale of economic activities means more elements of society and regions are excluded from productive participation in economic activity, except as consumers. And even that role is threatened by cuts to the social safety net in many industrialized countries. Whole regions, including their communities and residents, are becoming expendable.

By contrast, the local economy is one where enterprises respond to the issues, conditions and needs of the immediate community. Local enterprises, which share the fate of the community, are more sensitive to local requirements and conditions than a branch plant or subsidiary of a transnational whose headquarters is in some distant city. This is of special significance for communities undergoing economic difficulties. Where the local economy is successful, the question of where ownership rests, or where more specialized, more knowledge-intensive activities are concentrated does not matter as much. It is when a community is in trouble economically that the absence of local enterprises hurts because it means it has fewer resources with which it can respond.[3]

Technology can be a cause of local decline, but it can also pose a possible solution. Information technologies are a case in point. These include computers and automated information management and related technologies such as scanning, software and databases. Communications technologies are telephone-based transmission of digital messages. In the early days, digital transmission was primarily the property of proprietary networks, like the computer-based information moving along secure and dedicated networks from remote terminals to centralized mainframes. These networks, once found only in governments, the military and larger corporations, are now being superseded, in public consciousness and in reality, by personal computers and the Internet—or what is termed the "Information Highway."

The Internet itself started as a private network for facilitating communication within small scientific communities, particularly those engaged in defense-related research. Funded by the Defense research budget (DARPA), the Internet at first consisted of small electronic (e-mail) links within a small community of American physical scientists. Over the years, these connections spread to link scientists from various disciplines and communities throughout the United States. From there, as graduate students sought to maintain this electronic contact, the network extended even further, into the non-scientific community. By the early 1990s, it linked several thousand computers interacting as a single telephone-based network.[4]

In the early 1990s, a researcher with CERN, the particle physics laboratory in Geneva, wrote a computer language which could transmit graphic images via the Internet. This code, HTML (Hypertext Mark-Up Language), became the basis of the World Wide Web. Through its attractiveness, ease of use and placement of it in the public domain by the author Tim Berners-Lee, HTML revolutionized the way in which information is managed and communicated electronically.[5] The widespread access by a general and highly-dispersed audience to this information-processing and communications capability has brought technology and communications to people in rural and remote areas and to those otherwise technology-disadvantaged.

The Net can be used for one-to-one communication (e-mail), one-to-many communication (on-line webcasting and WWW presentation), many-to-many communication (electronic conferencing), and many-to-one communication (on-line democratic participation, and electronic commerce.) Bypassing conventional telephone networks, made possible by either satellite or cellular communication, means that people in rural and remote areas have the same access as do those in more central, favoured locations. The technology can provide the means for low-cost information distribution, and for electronic commerce and sales around the globe.

It may require us to modify how information-intensive activities are distributed; it may, for example, make it possible to decentralize information-intensive public sector activities and equalize employment opportunities. ICT also brings significant opportunities and advantages to local enterprises, in that it reduces the barriers of distance and location. ICT challenges accepted wisdom that urban concentration is an inevitable accompaniment of globalization because it makes distance less important, and so makes ownership and management of local information possible. Local businesses retain the flexibility of small-scale production and distribution.

Technology is reducing the cost of transmission, management and processing of information, and of any information-intensive undertaking. Better, more cost-effective education is possible irrespective of location.

The dream/vision of the "information society" has largely been a winners' dream. The real applications of technology—how it would actually work in the local economy—have largely been left to business and technology mavens to articulate. What the new wired world might look like for everyone else—that is, for those who will not necessarily be its beneficiaries—has been left largely unexplored.

We should not see ICT as inevitably leading to local economic development (LED); nor should we assume that it is a necessary ally of LED. Rather, ICT is a double-edged sword, slicing away barriers to the free flow of jobs and capital and, thus, local economic well-being. But for local businesses, it also carves a way to survival as their traditional economic base declines. ICT confers even to those in the most remote communities an astounding range of information development opportunities previously unavailable.

Technological change has, of course, taken its toll on local economies. Local economies, like all others, are being restructured by concentration and centralization of schools, hospitals and the service functions of large organizations. The result is less local demand, less public sector resource investment, the hollowing out and the de-skilling of local economies.

The skills needed for ICT are acquired through technical training or technical tinkering. In both rural and urban settings, these skills often devalue the traditional skills that once supported local economies. Thus, telephone companies' use of electronic polling for fault testing reduces the need for local line maintenance and repair. The loss of these and similar jobs has reduced the number of workers with job-related skills (and skill-related incomes) in local communities.

Unequal access to ICT is likely to become one of the major determinants of social and economic life in non-metropolitan (and metropolitan) areas. As more of the productive economy becomes integrated and infused with ICT, any limitation to access to technology, or to the training required to use ICT, will spell social and economic inequality between the "information-rich" and the "information-poor." ICT is today's means of production, just as were the tools of the early craft workers or the machines of the industrial age of production. Without access to these tools, whether restriction be physical, financial or educational, individuals and communities are restricted.

In many areas, local merchants are now threatened by the big-box merchants: local manufacturing firms are forced into competition with larger, non-local companies; and local production is transferred to lower-cost locations, generally offshore. Moreover, local investment dries up as local banks (in the US) or credit facilities (elsewhere) become absorbed by larger financial institutions. Investment shifts to locations which promise the highest short-term return, and away from local communities where return comes over a longer term.

ICTs give local communities and enterprises an historic opportunity to participate remotely, but directly, in the global economy as suppliers of specialty items and participants in production networks, as information processors and suppliers. Local enterprises can use the entire information network to become globalized. The network, at least for the moment, is open to everyone. Smoothly integrated communications networks allow businesses and individuals to transform local into national and national into global enterprises.

The promise of the microcomputer is the promise of decentralization. Concentration of computing power, and of the technical resources to support it, characterized the earlier mainframe era. Today, personal computers allow for enormously powerful, yet decentralized, computing—not only for those who can afford specialized technical support, but also for local and rural users. Commentators have repeatedly noted the economic empowerment and decentralizing opportunity that the PC revolution has created.

ICT may support local economies in remote working, or "telework." Decentralized computing capacity, when linked to a communications capacity like the Internet and through dedicated data lines, means that work can be done from any remote, networked location. This means there is an opportunity for remote access to skills and training. Thus, the playing field for technologically-oriented education and training is being leveled.

ICT also makes possible remote access to markets and suppliers, at least for some products. ICT is useful for the purchase of a variety of services, such as travel reservations and auto rentals. The already rapid growth in Internet purchasing, particularly of computer equipment, software and peripherals, suggests there is a ready market.

Theorists have extrapolated the positive and negative implications of technological change. A growing community of individuals and organizations are actively working to ameliorate the effects of technology change: to create communities with fiscal sustainability, reduced poverty and local control of the economy. These visionaries are using the new technologies to support local economic development in a number of ways:

1) by enabling local residents to do the work they have always done, better, faster, cheaper, or more efficiently, and thus maintaining their competitive position in the larger economic context;

2) as a resource for new businesses, new styles of development, and new initiatives, doing things at the local level which have not been done before and which may make a base for local economic advance; and

3) as a means to join larger networks, so that local economic activity which might not be competitive if undertaken in a piecemeal way, can become so.

The Net can be a marketing tool for small rural businesses; local entrepreneurs like Bed-and-Breakfast owners, hammock makers and lobster brokers can develop a Website and increase their market. These successes will likely grow in number as the Web expands. So far however, evidence of such success is anecdotal. In rural areas, the Net can be used as a tool for product or marketing information or for collaborative business activities like production and marketing. A current project of the University College of Cape Breton's Centre for Community and Enterprise Networking (C\CEN), contracted to the Federal Department of Industry, is to explore the use of the Internet as a business information tool for small businesses in rural Nova Scotia. To date, it appears that small rural businesses' interest in the technology is only limited.

The technology is also mobilizing a much wider, and more sophisticated range of resources to support local economic development initiatives than has ever before been possible. Music making and performance has become one of the most significant local industries in Cape Breton. Organizing performances and marketing performers, music schools and publications are activities that are migrating to the Internet. Internet access means that more of the benefits from this industry stay in Cape Breton.

A more difficult question is how to catalyze and elaborate on these successes, and how to develop new ideas and enterprises (rather than simply marketing existing ones).

ICT supports the formation of on-line networks for economic development. The technology allows for continuous communication, work-sharing and seamless presentation and marketing to the world of multiple centres as a single entity. It is like the highly successful "flexible networking" model found at work in Emilia-Romagna in Italy or in the United States' Appalachia (ACEnet).[6]

How to co-ordinate production and use the larger capacities of the network for more elaborate activities are also being explored. This research could be of major interest to local economies previously limited by lack of access to specialized skills and by their dispersed populations. Flexible networks are enriched by geographic or cultural social distinctiveness, and by being a part of a larger network of producers, even when the linkages are largely virtual.

A virtual (electronic) network could, for practical purposes, function as a virtual enterprise, taking advantage of the operational changes the technology affords. A virtual firm could optimize the advantages of ICTs distance insensitivity, local ownership of local information and the lower costs in rural locations. Networked enterprises could take advantage of network synergies by creating virtual cities and flexible, highly resilient small run production/processing, for information industries among others. This should create economies of disaggregation, rather than economies of scale.

New types of networked organizations may be created, structured as hubs and multiple self-sufficient nodes. Collaborative specialization, information dispersal and multiple or distributed ownership, decentralized and horizontal support structures, and a high degree of local self-sufficiency (and thus structural redundancy/survivability)—all characterize these new organizations. Clients' needs, geographical and cultural, can be responded to more immediately, thereby creating powerful and globally competitive marketing opportunities.

Many organizations are working diligently to use the new technology for local economic development, to build community networks and community access sites, and to develop local economic development agencies. Networks are most successful because they combine the technology's resources with local capabilities, and they do so in flexible, creative structures.

The earliest innovators in the use of the Net for "civilian" purposes were academic users. They were accustomed to electronic communication, and they took this knowledge with them when they moved outside of the formal and professional communication environments of the University. These early public-access networks developed idealistically, as ways of bringing computing to the people and operated as "freenets" or community networks without charge to the users. They were publicly accessible Internet networks providing Internet access for geographically defined communities, usually neighborhoods, where many university students and junior faculty were living.

These community networks carried primarily private electronic mail or information on voluntary and community activities. There were quite strict, if informal, injunctions against using the Net for commercial purposes. Only with widespread access to the Net, and the beginnings of the need to charge for its use, did commercial elements begin to creep into online communication.

Commercial applications of the Net really only began with the advent of the World Wide Web as a mass-market distributor of information, particularly because of its heavy reliance on attractive graphics. The recent development of electronic commerce ("e-commerce") applications is shifting the Net from a free to a commercial venture.

At first, local networks were concerned with community applications, but these were not tied to community or local economic development (CED/LED) efforts. There has been little overlap either in efforts or in personnel between CED/LED and Community Networking (CNs).[7] The proponents and developers of CNs disseminate community information, but they have apparently not seen the connection between the Net and community economic development, despite globalization and local job loss.

Consistent with its tradition of using public means to support social goals, Canada has begun to ensure technology access in areas and for populations which might not have it otherwise. The Federal Government, through the Department of Science and Industry, has launched the Community Access Program (CAP) which provides a one-time grant to rural communities who want Internet access. Initially, this programme was to provide raw Internet access, i.e. "Internet Points of Presence" in small and isolated rural communities where there might be no commercial information service provider.[8]

Commercial providers have, however, increased the range and scope of their activities and few communities have no commercial Internet access. The CAP Program now appears to be shifting its concern to ensuring broad "social" (in addition to physical) access, for those who, because of cost or other factors, might be denied use of the technology. CAP now provides public access to Internet terminals in schools, libraries, community centres or other community sites such as fire halls and grocery stores. Public sites like these are becoming known as "Telecentres."

The original 350 Community Access sites across rural Canada have quadrupled to 1,500, with an ultimate target of 5,000 nationally and an additional 5,000 in urban areas. Not incidentally, universal "public" access will allow governments to equitably deliver information or services cost-effectively via the Internet. In many communities (particularly in Atlantic Canada), the technology was launched at a time when other economic resources were in severe decline, and where the national system of broad social supports appeared to be under threat. The CAP Program and, through it, community Internet access quickly came to be seen not simply as a communication/information tool but also as a new instrument or resource for local economic development.

At Community Access'96, a conference hosted by UCCB's Centre for Community and Enterprise Networking (C\CEN), the focus of discussion was not what had originally been anticipated, issues of technical accessibility. Rather, it was how this new communications instrument might be used for economic development in rural communities where other instruments and resources were in decline. The conference delegates were representatives from local Community Access Committees in a broad cross-section of small town and rural Atlantic Canadians—with not one information professional among them. The issues that concerned them were whether the Net could be used to market local tourism attractions, how their sites could link with local small businesses, and what economic development opportunities might be available now that they were on the Net.[9]

In Nova Scotia, it became government policy to promote direct links among local economic development authorities and community access sites/projects. CAP was also classified as an "economic development" programme rather than as a communications support programme. Giving additional resources to support Community Access sites was justified as a contribution to local economic development rather than as support for continuing education.[10]

Access to a local post-secondary educational institution is a most significant resource if a community is to take advantage of technological opportunities. Such an institution can provide training for local residents and marketing knowledge to help local enterprises expand. Without it, communities may lack the knowledge, experience and confidence to respond to global challenges.

Especially through the Chair in the Management of Technological Change (MOTC), UCCB has been particularly active in encouraging community involvement. The Chairs in MOTC are sponsored by the National Science and Engineering and Social Science and Humanities Research Councils "to encourage study, teaching and training on how technological change and entrepreneurship can best be understood, managed and facilitated." UCCB is the smallest institution with a Chair, and the only one where the Chair programme is not linked to a major industrial sponsor with an active commercial interest in the programme.

Most Chairs of MOTC in this programme are in major

metropolitan centres and research universities. The Chair at UCCB is exceptional in that it is located in an undergraduate teaching university and in a non-metropolitan region. Moreover, it is in a region which is experiencing severe economic decline, and where persistent unemployment is unlikely to decrease since its fishing industry, steel plant and coal mines have to undergo further rationalizations.

The Associate Chair at UCCB, whose co-sponsor is Enterprise Cape Breton Corporation (ECBC), is directly concerned with responding to local problems by finding ways to replace employment being lost in traditional sectors with jobs in technology. The immediate research challenge of the ECBC Associate Chair is to respond to the employment needs in fishing and industrial communities, among young people who want to work and stay in their communities, and among older unemployed who need retraining to be able to return to useful work.

What the Chair in MOTC brings to the region is flexibility and responsiveness to immediate problems, access to the range of resources available through the University, and an objective outsider's perspective. In an economic and cultural context where there are few opportunities for experimentation and "research," and not much contact with outside influences, the Chair provides a stimulating addition to the local resource pool.[11]

The Associate Chair has exercised its responsibility through the establishment of a research, development and enterprise incubation centre, The Centre for Community and Enterprise Networking (C\CEN). The rationale for the Centre is that even where people are aware of the opportunities presented by ICT, they need specific activities and enterprises to take advantage of those opportunities. The Associate Chair MOTC started C\CEN in the summer of 1996. The Centre is intending to apply the new technologies to community-based economic development in Cape Breton.

The Associate Chair MOTC has identified as a major problem, in the development of ICT-based enterprises in a non-metropolitan region such as Cape Breton, the lack of information infrastructure including trained personnel. Information-intensive activities tend to be concentrated in established centres, such as administrative or governmental hubs and research university centres. Without these activities, a region suffers from a scarcity of knowledge/information intensive enterprises. Thus to provide a base for enterprise creation, C/CEN must substitute or find replacements for skills and expertise.

In this regard, C\CEN has chosen to focus on community applications of ICT for non-metropolitan areas—"rural informatics"—and include the technical and application supports for these activities. C\CEN has been investing to bring certain staff up to the state of the art, technologically speaking. This is not research in the traditional sense—of advancing the limits of the technology. Rather, it involves making a one-time only investment to ensure that the region can stay in the global economic game.

Where other available economic resources have failed, Cape Breton communities see ICT as offering some hope for sustainability. In this region, people must find new kinds of livelihoods, different from the resource-based employment of the past. If not, large-scale migration to urban centres, with the family disruption and loss of support networks that it invariably entails, is virtually certain.

C\CEN is conducting research in the design and delivery of remotely managed government services, particularly in how they could provide opportunities for contracting services to communities in Cape Breton. In addition, C\CEN is providing developmental and incubation support to several enterprises that want to provide contractual services remotely via the Internet; these businesses would capitalize on lower overhead costs and readier access to employment support programmes that could give them a possible competitive edge. Also, the Centre is examining ways to provide services and technical support to the not-for-profit and community sectors in information technology.

C\CEN acts as a catalyst for new developments. Its style is to experiment and build. In the process, C\CEN has developed a new style of local economic development—one that focuses on network building, hands-on learning and experimentation. In this case, the technology enables not just local economic development work; it also identifies new opportunities in technology and then works to develop these as local employment opportunities.[12]

One legacy of the resource extraction industries, which have sustained the Cape Breton economy for 200 years, is reluctance to recognize that work which does not involve physical effort can be an appropriate aspiration for local young people. A corollary of that reluctance is the expectation that local efforts and development must be linked to the primary resource sector.

Cape Bretoners have been skeptical about whether information technology-intensive enterprises could be successful. To move the economy to rely on ICT, it has been necessary to influence the local attitudes about work and about what could be accomplished in the community.

Through its monthly meetings, The Technology Advisory Group (TAG) has had a remarkable influence in changing local attitudes. The TAG, which is sponsored by UCCB through the Senior Chair MOTC and by ECBC, provides a technology showcase for the general community. Meeting time is provided for the presentation of technology and enterprise-oriented information and experiences, for announcements and for distributing promotional or support materials. Not incidentally, time is also reserved for socializing and developing contacts.

The TAG has been active for four years and has a mailing list of 600 participants. It also has regular monthly meetings where average attendance exceeds 100. The original TAG has spawned similar groups interested in the Culture and Heritage area (CHAG), and similar efforts in several other smaller Nova Scotia communities. The TAG has had the effect of creating a commercial ICT culture, a belief that things can be done in technology, even in a relatively remote area.

C\CEN has been particularly active in developing the support structure for a network of community access sites throughout rural Nova Scotia. In conjunction with the provincial Department of Education and with funding from the federal Department of Industry and four other Federal and Provincial agencies, C\CEN established a summer programme to hire 60 students to work throughout rural Nova Scotia to link small businesses, young people and the general public to the Internet through public Internet Access sites. CAP sites were targeted, but libraries and schools with Internet access were also included. The programme was called "Wire Nova Scotia"—WiNS.[13]

The programme went well. Over 3,000 people were trained in Internet access. Public Internet access programmes were organized in 40 rural communities around Nova Scotia. Several workers were offered more permanent work, while others decided to reorient their work aspirations. A public access/training programme was developed for people with disabilities, and a Virtual Centre for Cape Breton Music was initiated.

Most of the student workers went back to their respective schools and, in a few instances, agreements have been negotiated with income support agencies (Social Services, Unemployment Insurance, TAGS—an unemployed fisherman's transition programme) to allow those agencies' "clients" to replace the students as "volunteers." Through the system of regional coordinators and the electronic network set up to manage WiNS, some Internet and community access training was provided to the "volunteers."

This project was done with virtually no new money; its financing came from the redirection of existing (and committed) expenditures and energies. Indications are that some of the sites may make these arrangements more permanent by finding ways that the sites might generate revenue, or by redirecting to this project funds currently allocated to industrial development or tourism.

The development of the WiNS network as a human resource complement to the emerging network of community access sites in Nova Scotia is the initial step in the development of a province-wide "flexible network." This network would link rural communities and rural enterprises for common marketing of goods and services, and for production and information processing.

A fledgling example of a "distributed flexible information management network" appears to be emerging in the rural Straits-East Nova area of the province. Collaboration by the local School Districts and the local regional economic development authority has created the SENCEN (Straits East Nova Community Enterprise Network), which is attempting to develop a "virtual city" in the Strait of Canso area of Eastern Nova Scotia. This project grew out of a successful Community Access site in a small fishing village. Here, a particularly entrepreneurial manager created a CAP site, which began to function as a kind of rural copy shop—with e-mail/Internet access, a variety of software tools and training, and other small business supports. The Community Enterprise Network (CEN) was adopted by the community and became a hub of training and small business activity for the area, doing job searches, web-site development for marketing, contract computer training and some remote technical service provision.[14]

The site inspired several people in the region to consider linking other regional CAP sites and to make use of surplus space in local schools. In addition, there was the suggestion that WiNS could be extended by taking on volunteer managers/trainers/outreach workers (currently unemployed individuals) and arranging for them to continue to receive their unemployment insurance or support programmes while being trained/working in the CEN.

SENCEN is pioneering the development of a telework experiment, an information technology purchasing co-operative for community access sites, and a fledgling network-based commercial enterprise to compete for information management contracts in the marketplace.

The development of small- or medium-sized private enterprises, using ICT as a resource for their business, is an objective and a link in the chain of developing and redeveloping a local economy. While many small and medium-sized businesses use computers, the actual use of ICT to develop a new enterprise demonstrates the success of the rebuilding of the local economy.

Cape Breton has seen a number of such successes, including several Web design and development firms, award-winning multimedia companies and several small software firms. In each case, these entrepreneurs have had to invest in developing and maintaining their technical skills at a high level in order to compete for off-Island business.

A key element in developing and maintaining ICT businesses in the Cape Breton economy has been support networks of individuals and small firms. A consortium of firms, MediaFusion, was established initially as a lobby group for the sector, as a way of marketing the skills of individuals and small firms to better compete for larger projects. That latter effort raised the profile of the sector, and provided a means for professionalizing the activity, through training, role modeling and mentoring and by linking individual enterprises into larger off-Island networks and activities. All of this has contributed substantially to the local successes in the sector.[15]

The initial broad coalition of MediaFusion is in the process of evolving into a smaller and more focussed ICT sector business incubator, "Silicon Island," to be located in Sydney, Cape Breton. A number of small businesses in the sector will share services and staff, and will give the joint marketing and presentation a physical presence. Local networks like these achieve substantial synergies, as firms share information, moral support, contacts and services to carry out larger export contracts.

ICT, particularly the Internet, is offering benefits/opportunities to some—better marketing of tourism operations and specialized products such as crafts or foodstuffs, and full- or part-time telework from a rural or remote setting. Training and job searches, sophisticated assessments of local opportunities and limitations—all of these can be pursued locally.

Though some applications are selective and primarily for those few that already have access to the technology, their overall effect is to improve the local infrastructure to a point and ultimately make community-based economic development a reality.

The role of ICT in local/rural economic development is still, however, very much in flux. There are many experiments and initiatives. We are only just beginning to apply the technology in practical activities. While it is evident that the technology does decentralize information-intensive activities to non-metropolitan areas, barriers remain for regions wanting to use ICT. Among them are the absence of a skilled workforce, the inadequacy of the local ICT infrastructure and the inevitable inertia of metropolitan administrations to transfer significant functions to relatively remote locales.

Whether the technology actually helps business in rural areas, or whether it ultimately accelerates their decline by advertising larger metropolitan suppliers, remains to be determined.

In this area, where the reliance on resource extraction increases even as the economy founders, ICT infrastructure development and experimentation is certainly warranted. The only alternative is continuing rural depopulation and metropolitan concentration.

ENDNOTES

1. The impact that ICT is having on the commercial and financial marketplace is being very widely discussed. The work of William Greider, *One World, Ready or Not: The Manic Logic of Global Capitalism*, New York: Simon & Schuster, 1997 and Bill Gates' self-congratulatory *The Road Ahead*, Rockland, MA: Viking Press, 1995 and the ongoing discussion of the issues in the *Economist* Magazine might be noted.

2. The other side of the globalization discussion is also extremely active currently particularly around issues such as the likely impact of the Multilateral Agreement on Investment (MAI) and the World Trade Organization. For a good introduction to some of the discussion see David Korten, *When Corporations Rule the World.* Berrett-Koehler Pub./Kumarian Press, 1996, and the work of Tony Clarke and Maude Barlow and others, as indexed in the World Wide Web site: http://mai.flora.org/library/keywordlist.html

3. Michael Gurstein, "Managing Technology for Non-Metropolitan Development: A Case Study of Cape Breton Island," UNIG Conference Proceedings, UNESCO Conference on Management of Technology, Istanbul, Turkey, 1996.

4. For a very useful history of the Internet, see Michael and Ronda Hauben, *Netizens: On the History and Impact of Usenet and the Internet.* Los Alamitos, CA: IEEE Computer Society, 1997.

5. A history of the World Wide Web can, of course, be found on the WWW. See: "Brief History <http://www.ug.ecs.soton.ac.uk/~mkt95/cm316.html>-Dec '97.-

6. Michael Gurstein, Applying the Concept of *"Flexible Networks"* to Community Access Computing, unpublished ms.

7. The most comprehensive book available on Community Networking is Douglas Schuler's *New Community Networks: Wired for Change*, New York: Addison Wesley, 1995.

8. The "official" Community Access Program web-site is at http://cap.unb.ca/

9. The proceedings of the Community Access'96 conference may be found at <http://ccen.uccb.ns.ca/ca96/>

10. *A Vision for Community Access in Nova Scotia*, Nova Scotia Community Access Committee, Halifax, nd.

11. Gurstein, Ibid.

12. C\CEN's website, http://ccen.uccb.ns.ca has descriptions of most of its major projects.

13. The WiNS website. http://ccen.uccb.ns.ca/wins contains useful descriptive information about the project. See also Sally Lerner et. al., *An Evaluation of Wire Nova Scotia 1996*, nd., C\CEN Occasional Paper 1; Michael Gurstein and Kristin Andrews, *A Summary Report on Wire Nova Scotia 1996*, nd., C\CEN Occasional Paper 2; and Bruce Dienes, *A Summary Report on Wire Nova Scotia, 1997* nd., C\CEN Occasional Paper 3, Sydney, NS.

14. The activities of SENCEN are described in <http://sencen.ednet.ns.ca>

15. MediaFusion's description and other documents may be found in <http://www.mediafusion.ca/>

10

Community Economic Development and Persons with Disabilities: A Case Study and Critical Issues for Organizations

Scott MacAulay

In the aftermath of the British election in 1997, BBC Radio 4 carried a story about a long-time Labour Party supporter who, on the day of the vote, went to the polling station with great excitement in anticipation of the expected Labour victory. The polling station was only accessible by going up a flight of stairs, which he could not do because he was in a wheelchair. He insisted on voting and arrangements were made for him to vote in the not-so-private setting of the parking lot. The story included interviews with disability organization representatives who said that the vast majority of their members would not have had the self-confidence to insist. They would have simply turned around and gone home.

This story is a reminder that the rights we have on paper are not always the rights we have in practice. There are barriers, both physical and social, which stifle or block the sound of certain voices being heard, and which, in the end, can discourage people from even trying to speak. Persons with disabilities[1] experience these barriers everyday, and thus many of their rights as citizens are illusory. When a flight of stairs is the only entry to many public and commercial buildings, and when a public transportation system makes only a token number of buses or trains accessible, we have a *de facto* system of *apartheid*.[2] The movement of a particular social group is curtailed and limited.

It is because of this system of *apartheid* that persons with disabilities began to organize in the late 1960s and early 1970s. Spurred on by other civil rights movements, they began to critically examine the extent of their equality as citizens. The politics of disability moved beyond disparate single issues and reliance on non-disabled experts for advocacy, to the general social environment as systematically biased against persons with disabilities. Reliance on system-sponsored experts was part of the problem, not part of the solution. These changes can now be argued to locate the disabled people's collective activity among those late twentieth-century "new social movements" which no longer seek change through party political systems or along the usual pressure-group lines.[3]

As Oliver argues, the disability movement and other new social movements are "culturally innovative in that they are part of the underlying struggles for genuine participatory democracy, social equality and justice, which have arisen out of the crisis in industrial culture."[4] The crisis is one in which the inherent logic of capitalism to influence the creation of cultural homogeneity is challenged by the politics of difference, of identity.[5]

The struggle for participatory democracy meant the emergence of organizations run by, not for, persons with disabilities. These organizations pursued structural political and economic changes and the destruction and reconstruction of public attitudes to persons with disabilities through advocacy and awareness-raising. Viewed from a community development perspective, the disability movement can be considered part of the "progressive tradition," which integrates social and economic objectives "as part of a strategy of basic social change."[6]

In the late 1990s, statistics confirm the need for continued struggle. Eighty percent of adults with disabilities in Canada are unemployed.[7] A report released by the Government of Nova Scotia stated that the "degree of sexual abuse of people with disabilities is at least 150 percent of that for individuals of the same sex and age without disabilities."[8]

The community development initiative discussed in this chapter relates to the efforts of persons with disabilities to organize more effectively to improve their ability to secure employment and to engage in direct economic activity through entrepreneurship. The initiative is to establish a Centre of Excellence in Entrepreneurship and Technology in the Cape Breton Regional Municipality, in Sydney, Nova Scotia. The Centre will use technology as an information, education and employment resource for persons with disabilities.

While the focus is on persons with disabilities, the underlying purpose of the chapter is to raise issues and questions for marginalized groups to consider when organizing for community development. These will be drawn from the discussion presented above, using the case of the Centre of Excellence as a reference point. Critical commentary is integrated with the telling of the Centre's story. The commentary, to reiterate, is not meant to be an evaluation of the Centre itself. The Centre provides a backdrop for the author's presentation of fundamental theoretical considerations for community development. These theoretical considerations challenge the rhetoric of mainstream community development apologists which states that simply because people live in the same geographic area they have the same political, social and economic interests in social change. Communities, reflecting the broader social environment in which they have to function, are characterized at least as much by systemic conflict as they are by the potential to reach consensus about the end goals of community development.

There is tension between a social movement, aimed at

long-term cultural transformation, and the task of initiating projects locally, with limited resources, to meet short-and medium-term needs—access to work, shelter, transportation, and so on. Too many compromises in the latter can contradict the long-term goals of the social movement by weakening solidarity with the social movement beyond the community. Community development's strength, however, is that it can avoid unnecessary abstraction. It deals with real people in real places who interact daily, potentially bringing together people from different backgrounds to work on practical projects that could enhance people's quality of life right away. The case described here reflects this tension.

COMMUNITY INVOLVEMENT OF THE DISABLED

Community Involvement of the Disabled, or CID, is an organization of persons with disabilities in the Cape Breton Regional Municipality. The organization consists of persons with a range of physical and mental disabilities. CID was established in 1974 as a non-profit society. Its working philosophy is based on what is known as the consumer movement, a movement which states that it is persons with disabilities who know best what is required to meet their needs in such areas as housing, transportation, education and social programmes. The philosophy is in stark contrast to the still-too-common idea that persons with disabilities are, or ought to be, wards of the state—reliant on social workers, medical personnel and special needs educators to dictate what is best for them.

The early history of CID provides many success stories about initiating local change and being a driving force in the consumer movement in Nova Scotia and in the nation. A few examples are:

In 1978, locally, it won the establishment of a specialized transportation system for persons with disabilities who could not access the regular bus system in this area.

In 1979, it was instrumental in forming a provincial organization dedicated to the consumer movement.

In 1981, it played a leading role in lobbying the federal government to include persons with disabilities in the Canada Human Rights Act.

In sum, the early years of CID were a flurry of activism, including one protest march, blocking downtown traffic for several hours, to protest the provincial Building Code. These successes are in keeping with Bickenbach's summation of the disability movement in this time period:

> "The disablement social movement of the 1970s and the 1980s was notable for its focus on self-help and self-empowerment. Although the movement expressed its demands in the language of equality rights, it also pursued various forms of direct political action, such as sit-ins and boycotts, demonstrations and lobbying activities."[9]

From the mid-1980s on, CID settled in with its hard-won legitimacy, having secured federal government funding for an employment outreach officer, which, along with a much smaller percentage of local contributions, provided for comfortable office space and the resources to underwrite services to members. CID concentrated on being a watchdog to make sure that previous victories were not threatened; sending regular newsletters to inform members of internal news and provincial and national issues; and generally having board and membership meetings, sending representatives to provincial and national conferences and all the busyness that entails. In terms of service to all members, the main concrete benefit was in the area of recreation. CID put great effort into sponsoring dances, special event parties and, in 1990, establishing a bowling league for persons with disabilities. An unforeseen consequence of the focus on recreation was that by the mid-1990s, the average member of CID, not involved at the board level, thought of the organization as one which provided the opportunity for an outing from time to time, not as an effective political voice in the struggle for real equality.

There is a contradiction here. The dynamics of social movements and community development are often characterized by an initial struggle to gain legitimacy as an alternative vision *within* the community. Yet, forces external to the community, which are identified as barriers to achieving the alternative vision, can turn around and sanction the process before it is fully developed and accepted by the majority of stakeholders; these forces can pose a real challenge to the status quo. For instance, limited concessions from the government ("the state"), like legislative changes, that give access to state resources through targeted programmes can create dependency and thus complacency and conservatism. Members then tend to shy away from rocking the boat. The leaders of organizations can become more occupied with maintaining legitimacy in the eyes of the state than in the eyes of the social groups they serve and are a part of—an occupation which ultimately contributes to a hegemonic system in which certain social groups are marginalized. This suggests the importance of organizations having an ongoing commitment to critical analysis, as part of a social movement, as a guide to action. This critical analysis needs to be generated by those who are marginalized, and kept vibrant and alive through popular and democratic education programmes; first for the grassroots membership and, only secondarily, for the community at large and its hegemonic institutions. To quote Bickenbach again:

> By its nature, counter-hegemonic politics is far more revolutionary than political agitation directed at specific legislative or political ends.

> The aim of the former is to attack, directly and dramatically, a dominant societal framework, rather than to use it and the social institutions that make it up in order to win favourable concessions.[10]

In 1994, CID elected a new president, a graduate of the University College of Cape Breton with a degree in Business Administration. The president of CID was to play a key role in the establishment of the Centre of Excellence. Recognizing the dramatically-changing environment in government funding because of the battle to cut debts and deficits, the president was well aware of the fact that any organization that did not adapt was not likely to survive. The federal and provincial governments began encouraging non-profit organizations throughout Canada to embark on strategic planning processes aimed at clarifying organizational objectives, increasing efficiency and eventually achieving sustainability. Decoded ideologically, "sustainability" meant being able to survive without the welfare state, becoming entrepreneurial by instituting revenue-generating services or, perhaps more realistically, competing for private sector and charitable support, or simply lowering the level of service to members.

The new president was also aware of the technological advancements in assistive devices and information technology, which might reduce the high unemployment rate among persons with disabilities, a reality she herself had experienced despite her education. CID faced a potential economic crisis; at the same time, its leader was equipped to address the economic barriers members faced. Her competence promised that CID might be made relevant to the day-to-day lives of its members.

The disability movement in Canada has made great gains in independent living in the past 20 years in accessibility, education and recreation. Yet the struggle to achieve economic independence continues, and it is especially difficult in areas of high unemployment such as Cape Breton. The question here is: How can the goals of a politics of identity be achieved without full and meaningful employment? In a capitalist society, the ability to fully participate as a citizen is tied to meaningful and well-paid employment. Patterns of high unemployment among certain social groups make farcical the promise of citizenship, theoretically accorded to all. This issue is more problematic in peripheral regions, where persons with disabilities have to compete with able-bodied people for jobs. Politically, it is hard for persons with disabilities to be heard because the majority (able-bodied unemployed people) may feel threatened if special status or initiatives are provided to "special interest groups." Moreover, persons with disabilities are underdeveloped as a class, having very limited experience working for owners of the means of production. In terms of securing the skills and political clout that, at least potentially, rest within in the working class, persons with disabilities face an uphill battle. This battle is something they have in common with some other new social movements; and this calls for solidarity and dialogue with progressive organizations of women, First Nations and others. It means working together to dismantle barriers and create positive social change, and avoiding the trap of competing with each other for the crumbs of a disintegrating welfare state. Linking community development and social movements, Shragge argues:

> "CED [community economic development] organizations cannot become isolated, but in order to attain their goals of addressing poverty, they have to be engaged in the wider struggles for economic and social justice through alliances with organizations with similar interests."[11]

In 1995, CID secured money from the federal government to develop a five-year strategic plan. The funding was modest, paying only a facilitator to work with the Board of Directors and interested members for a period of three days. The author was hired as facilitator. A process was designed to allow participants, in small groups and plenary sessions, to identify CID's strengths and weaknesses, to formulate a vision statement to guide the organization for the next five years, and to articulate from that vision statement specific goals and the objectives that would meet them.[12] Reflecting the values of the consumer movement, the facilitator was not the expert brought in to tell CID what it needed.

The resultant plan had a total of 13 goals. Under each goal, there were from five to ten concrete objectives organized according to a timeline for completion. Many of the goals dealt with traditional areas of concern such as housing, transportation and recreation. But there was one goal which stood out as a priority for the coming years—the establishment of a Centre of Excellence for Technology and Entrepreneurship.

Economically, technology is especially relevant for persons with disabilities. The rapid advances in information and assistive device technologies can be harnessed by persons with disabilities, improving their employability potential by showing employers that hiring a person with a disability is possible without major changes to the physical working environment. As Roulstone points out:

> "The possibilities for employing disabled people who use technology should expand as their abilities are realised. Whilst attitudinal change should not be overstated, the practicalities of employing formerly excluded workers should become ever more obvious."[13]

Roulstone, however, goes on to argue that technology is

not enough. Persons with disabilities have been socialized to have low self-esteem. This means that however skilled in the application of information technology, for example, it will be a struggle for an individual to fill a position requiring autonomous intellectual analysis and decision making.

Technology also raises issues of identity for persons with disabilities. Zola states:

> "[T]echnology can do too much for those of us with disabilities. The machines that technology creates may achieve such completeness that they rob us of our integrity by making us feel useless...To be handled by a machine or animal, where once I was handled by a person, can only be invalidating of me as a person." [14]

Admittedly, Zola's perspective is a radical one. But it does underscore the fact that a positive sense of identity is tied to integrity—and that for persons with disabilities there needs to be awareness of the potential for the globalizing forces of technology to steal away with that integrity. Tech-utopian visions invite those forces in, especially in capitalist society where the dominant individualist ideology views technology for persons with disabilities as a way of compensating for individuals' inadequacies, making "them" the same as "us." The implicit message to persons with disabilities is: You are no good to anyone in your original state.

This, of course, does not mean the disability movement should advocate a Luddite-like dismissal of technology. The use of technology is a universal human trait. It does suggest, however, the need for the movement to take up a call for the socialization of the development and distribution of technology. This would allow for persons with disabilities to create technologies for themselves, thereby mitigating the loss of integrity. Persons with disabilities could use technology to remove social barriers, not to re-engineer individuals. It is significant in the case analyzed here that the project couples technology with entrepreneurship. This suggest, perhaps, a bias towards an analysis which views the economic issues of persons with disabilities as problematic for individuals, not the social movement, and not rooted in unjust social systems.

Shortly after the release of the strategic plan, the facilitator became associated with the Community Economic Development Institute at UCCB and maintained an active role as advisor to CID. This institute is idea-rich and cash-poor and could offer little in the way of funding for a more detailed analysis of the Centre of Excellence concept. However, UCCB had an Associate Chair in the Management of Technological Change which had a mandate to participate actively in technological change and study its implications in non-metropolitan areas. Persons with disabilities in non-metropolitan areas have challenges which those in large areas do not. There is not a critical mass of population to justify specialized centres of service. There are greater challenges to accessing capital and generating and disseminating information.[15] The Centre of Excellence addressed these challenges by planning to offer a range of services in what would essentially be a one-stop shop for accessing technology, employment and entrepreneurial support. The facilitator made some inquiries with the Associate Chair and advised CID to approach it for support in further developing the concept. The Associate Chair agreed.

The Associate Chair provided research money. It was decided that that money would be used to determine the need for the Centre and to get feedback from members on what services they wanted most. Using the Internet, similar models and programmes throughout North America were to be identified. A researcher was hired to work with an advisory committee of the Community Economic Development Institute and the Associate Chair in the Management of Technological Change.

The end result was an operational model for the Centre. It was not a detailed operational plan with programmes, costs, and revenue flows. The nucleus of a such a plan, however, was formed. The model described the general characteristics of the Centre, the services it would offer, and its sources of revenue. Characteristics included linkages to local businesses, educational institutions and government; governance by persons with disabilities; co-operation with other demographic groups in the region who could benefit from the services, especially seniors; support from volunteer technical advisors from UCCB and the private sector; and an ongoing community awareness-raising and public advocacy function.

The Centre's services included assessment of individual consumers on assistive devices that would aid in daily living; assessment of work sites to improve accessibility; the display and availability on a trial basis of the latest in assistive device technologies; training for persons with disabilities in information technology, entrepreneurship and job readiness; consulting services and workshops on employment equity; rental and rent-to-purchase agreements for information and assistive technologies; and the development of a peer lending programme to assist consumers in purchasing technologies.

The plan foresaw that economic viability of the Centre could be achieved through a fee-for-service; payment for consultation services to potential employers; agreements with the provincial government to provide assessment services to the Department of Education and the Workers Compensation Board; and agreements with federal and provincial economic development agencies to provide specialized services for persons with disabilities.

Significantly, the plan did not assume that relations with

the state were to be cut off; they were simply to be renegotiated. The state would not allocate resources to a marginalized group; rather, it would provide a fee for services rendered, out of which the organization would have to take a profit. In other words, as indicated above, the organization would have to be self-supporting. It would be a business first, and part of a social movement only if it could afford to be and could do so in a way which would not jeopardize business with the state. In such an arrangement, the state takes on the role of a potential customer, in a market place where it is one of the few potential customers with a substantial amount of money to spend. Thus despite the rhetoric of sustainability, the organization would remain dependent, and this would limit critical analysis. More concretely, the integration of counter-hegemonic social and economic objectives which characterizes progressive community development, as discussed above, is limited.

To increase its technical expertise, CID decided to expand the advisory committee to include private sector representation. SHL Systemhouse, a national information management firm, agreed to provide a person from its local operation. The research the Associate Chair had financed was used to prepare a proposal for funding for the Centre. That proposal included a budget of $105,000 for implementation personnel, overhead and research expenses. After months of meetings with different layers of government, contributions for that full amount were secured from the federal, provincial and municipal governments. A press conference announcing the project was held early in the spring of 1997.

Shortly thereafter, CID began hiring. A local law firm and accounting firm volunteered representatives to assist in screening suitable candidates. These representatives, along with a local bank manager, joined the advisory committee as partners to help CID oversee the implementation.

Representatives from the private and public sectors deepen the pool of human resources an organization can draw on. They also raise the political legitimacy of the project, which helps to secure financing. From the state's perspective, partnerships share costs and risks and generally lower the price an organization needs to charge for delivering government services through the volunteer donation of partners' skills. Partnerships also raise awareness among partners. In the Centre's case, the private sector representatives and those from UCCB might have gained insight into the consumer movement and the lived experiences of individual people with disabilities. Perhaps because of this, the fabric of civil society, locally, was made a little more accommodating to persons with disabilities. Likewise, through participation in meetings with lawyers, bankers, academics and others, some persons with disabilities may have become more comfortable with the jargon and procedures that can mystify and act as barriers to approaching the institutions these people represent.

Partnerships, however, are complex and unpredictable. It is difficult to know what really motivates the parties. In the case of the Centre of Excellence, the institutionally determined motivations of the partners might have been a mixture of charity, solidarity, potential financial gain, academic recognition or enhanced corporate image. Partnerships do not always mean unity of purpose. Different motivations can sometimes clash, with the organization the partnership is supposed to serve caught in the middle. Moreover, relations of power, direct and indirect, formal and informal, are inherent in social relations. The social relations that have historically marginalized a group can account for a perspective from which it views the partners' participation as an act for which the partners receive nothing in return—an act done out of kindness and empathy. Thus, the marginalized group can be in a state of permanent humility and gratitude, a disempowering state that does little to further a positive politics of identity and social change. It is here that critical analysis as a social movement has to come to the fore and inform a marginalized group's negotiation of partnerships and alliances for community development. If such an analysis is not present, the negotiations may simply produce structures which perpetuate inequality, albeit with a reconstructed ideology of consensus and inclusiveness.

One person in a wheelchair who argues at the foot of the stairs for the ability to vote, as well as those who would not argue, who would rather turn away in frustration, do not need charitable assistance, or enlightened compromise. They are not needy. They are people whose rights have been denied them. Likewise, ensuring full and free access to education, technology, and meaningful employment for persons with disabilities is not about sympathetic correction or compensation. It is about dismantling *apartheid* and removing the barriers to full citizenship. Community development can be one very important tool for doing this, but only if the disability movement as a social movement remains central to the process.

ENDNOTES

1. "Persons with disabilities" is the term used by the organization of persons who initiated the project referred to throughout this chapter. The argument for using it as opposed to "disabled person" is that it denotes a whole person who happens to have a disability, and does not suggest that his or her *person* be disabled. Within the disability movement, debates about language are vibrant. For example, Michael Oliver, a British sociologist who has a disability, is critical of the use of "persons with disabilities." "This liberal and humanist view flies in the face of reality as it is experienced by disabled people themselves who argue that far from being an appendage, disability is an essential part of the self. In this view it is nonsensical to talk about the person and the disability separately and consequently disabled people are demanding acceptance as they are, as disabled people." Oliver, Michael, *The Politics of Disablement*. London: Macmillan Press Ltd., 1990, p. xiii.

2. Mike Oliver and Colin Barnes, "Discrimination, disability and welfare: From needs to rights," in *Disabling Barriers - Enabling Environments*, edited by John Swain, Vic Finkelstein et al., London: Sage Publications, 1996.

3. Ibid. Ken Davis, "On the movement," in Oliver & Barnes, p. 285.

4. Ibid.

5. An excellent introduction to the politics of identity is found in Jonathan Rutherford, ed., *Identity: Community, Culture and Difference*. London: Lawrence and Wishart, 1990.

6. Eric Shragge, "Community Economic Development: Conflicts and Visions," in *Community Economic Development: In Search of Empowerment*. Eric Shragge, ed., Montréal: Black Rose Books, 1997, p. 11.

7. "Hiring Must Start" in "Focus on Ability: Changing the Way Canadians Think About Physical Disability," a special supplement to the *Globe and Mail*, February 13, 1998.

8. "Abuse of Disabled Concerns Officials," *The Cape Breton Post*, February 13, 1998, p. 3.

9. cited in Michael Oliver, "The Disability Movement is a New Social Movement", in *Community Development Journal*, Vol. 32, No. 3, 1997, p. 250.

10. Ibid.

11. Shragge, p. 16.

12. Scott MacAulay, *Look To the Future: Five Year Strategic Plan*. Sydney: Community Involvement of the Disabled, 1995.

13. Alan Roulstone, in Swain, Finkelstein et. al., eds. "Access to new technology in the employment of disabled people," p. 243.

14. Cited in Michael Oliver, 1990.

15. Patricia Flynn, *Centre of Excellence: Research Project Final Report* (Sydney: Chair in the Management of Technological Change, 1996).

PART 4

RESEARCH AND DEVELOPMENT IN COMMUNITY ECONOMIC DEVELOPMENT

11

Through A Glass Darkly: Looking for CED

Constance P. deRoche

In 1995, I agreed to sit on the board of the newly formed Community Economic Development (CED) Institute at the University College of Cape Breton (UCCB). I admired the work in which some of my colleagues, especially Greg MacLeod, had been involved for two decades. That work had led to the formation of a number of community development corporations (CDCs), the organizational instruments for CED action. Institute members played key roles in designing a Master's degree in Business Administration with a focus on CED. In successfully arguing their case for approval by the requisite external accreditation body, the programme's advocates pointed out that Cape Breton is a CED centre of national stature. New Dawn, the oldest CDC in Canada, is indeed seen as noteworthy in many published surveys,[1] and the work of Cape Breton activists has been included in major collections.[2] The UCCB Press recently began to publish local books about CED,[3] and the list of such publications is growing, as illustrated by the current volume. This groundswell, and my interest in how ordinary people cope with economic circumstance,[4] led me to cast a more academic eye on CED both locally and beyond my backyard.

As an interested observer, I had a broad, largely taken-for-granted understanding of the phenomenon. It was about local people, with no special political power or personal control of extraordinary resources, undertaking social action to stem the tide of decline that comes of being part of a wider economic system that, by its very nature, produces economic disparities. As I began to study it,[5] I soon discovered that the more specific meanings and practices of CED can vary widely. As I read and listened, the line between CED and "community development" work greyed. It paled as I compared projects identified as CED with similar ones to which the name is not applied. Likewise, as I observed the scene, the boundary between private-sector development and community-economic development became obscure. Now, I asked myself: What is CED? Such is research: it teaches you the limits of your knowledge, and it raises more questions than it answers. But is the question useful? *I* needed to know, but not all those I enlisted in my quest agreed that the question is useful.

To anthropologists, the actors are the experts. I wanted to talk to practitioners, especially those whose world views were not available in published form. I raised the question in numerous interviews, only to be met with puzzlement (as if to suggest, "you're the professor"), or the amused claim that there is no answer, or sympathy (by one who confessed her own struggle with the term). There was even impatience, from one activist who explained that it didn't matter, so long as the work was being done, and it had been going on since before the term was coined. Indeed, CED practice is often too all-consuming to leave time for debate, and "definitions" do abound.

The point of this chapter is *not* to provide a rarefied, abstract, exclusionary, "one-size-fits-all" definition, or even to mark boundaries. Like all fields of thought and action, community economic development is "socially constructed" and "emergent." Simply put, people create it, in their thinking, social discourse, and collective action. Cultural diversity and change are the products of all human social activity. In the folklore of anthropology, there is Sol Tax's definition of the discipline: anthropology is simply what anthropologists *do*. Extending this and applying it in the present context, we can say that CED is whatever is done in its name, or whatever its practitioners claim it to be. This, again, is diverse and non-consensual. But by exploring the meanings behind the different usages, we may be better able to think, talk, and assess rhetoric and practice.

A CED animator, hired to investigate grassroots interest in a district of the province, described how she would lead focus groups in various rural areas. To promote discussion, she typically asked group members to consider the "three little words" of which the term was comprised. Among scholars, of course, none of these words is little; individually each has provoked big debates.[6] It is not surprising, then, that the composite form should raise various complex issues. CED covers a spectrum of meanings ranging from quite traditional mainstream economic strategies to radically new ones. The following sections attempt to illustrate that spectrum.

NOVA SCOTIA: OPEN TO THE WORLD

This is the title of a periodical published by Atlantic Progress Publishing (that also produces *Atlantic Progress*, the official magazine of the Atlantic Provinces Chamber of Commerce). Its July 1997 issue, devoted to CED, was produced in co-operation with the province's Department of Economic Development and Tourism through the "co-operation and assistance of [its] Community Economic Development Division...and the regional development authorities [RDAs] across Nova Scotia."[7] The magazine reflects a perspective that helps us understand the range of CED meanings.

It contains, for example, a tear-out free subscription form which lures potential outside entrepreneurs by exhorting readers to: "Discover a province with endless possibilities... Learn why more and more business leaders are choosing Nova Scotia—for their companies, and their families...There's an opportunity on every page" of the issue. A note (in fine print, in a corner) advises that "The Publisher reserves the right to select only qualified recipients." Geography is not a criterion for qualification. The publication data note that the magazine is available "world-wide to qualified readers."[8] A brief questionnaire at the bottom reflects the target audience. It first asks respondents to specify "industry category," listing a number of manufacturing and service options (although general categories for "education," "government," and "non-profit organizations" are included). Another question, that asks for job function, lists "Owner/Executive Management," three other management roles, and an "other" category. The final question concerns the size of the budget that applicants manage, ranging from "under $500,000" to "over $10,000,000." Needless to say, this publication does not target the ordinary resident of Nova Scotian communities.

Another insert, from the Nova Scotia Marketing Agency, also reflects the magazine's agenda. It offers a checklist for requesting more information of two types: travel (e.g., Meetings and Convention) and business. The latter includes both "industries" (e.g., Environmental) and "opportunities" (e.g., Investment, Expansion, and Telephone Call Centre). Notably, Community Economic Development is listed in the business information group (but not in the Winter 1998 issue.) The brief questionnaire that follows is identical to that in the subscription form, except in one significant way. It specifically asks whether or not "your company plans to expand or open new facilities in the next three years."

The issue includes an advertisement by the Department of Economic Development and Tourism and for some of the

RDAs. Like the periodical's title itself, these ads reveal the tolerance range of public, officially endorsed CED discourse. First, though not exclusively targeted to outside entrepreneurs, they are designed in cognizance of that audience. The provincial department's ad notes that "Entrepreneurs and multinational corporations know the value of locating in Nova Scotia."[9] Some RDAs speak to the world by describing their districts: "Cumberland is located centrally in the Maritimes;"[10] "Pictou County, Nova Scotia, is home to some of Atlantic Canada's largest companies. It offers a strategic geographic location for your business;"[11] or "We invite you to explore Lunenburg and Queens Counties, Nova Scotia."[12] The Cumberland County RDA is especially direct, asking: "Are you interested in opening your own small business or relocating your multinational company?"[13]

The ads address standard private-sector concerns. Colchester is flagged as "North America's Best Value Site Selection" because of its location as a transportation and communications hub of the Atlantic provinces, and because of its "Low Cost, Very High Productivity Workforce, Low Facilities Development and Business Operating Costs."[14] Pictou boasts "a dynamic workforce, competitive operating costs, an abundance of natural resources and extensive community and government support."[15] Cumberland, in its forthright manner, offers both a "Dedicated and Reliable Workforce" and "Community Venture Equity Funds."[16] Lunenburg/Queens welcomes explorers who are looking "for lower operating costs, superior communications, an experienced work force, and a more relaxed lifestyle."[17] It offers "support services...[for] business start-ups and expansions, facilitation and information services, community planning, tourism and natural resource development."[18] These ads are reminiscent of Douglas' description of the industrial development strategies that were commonly used in the past by municipalities.[19]

References to "community" in these advertisements are few, and RDA work with local communities appears almost incidental. It is perhaps unfair to illustrate RDA involvements by focusing upon publicity from a periodical meant to market the province globally. While a survey of RDA activities across the province is well beyond the scope of this chapter, they clearly do engage in a breadth of community based undertakings. Indeed, they are mandated to organize, animate, co-ordinate, and serve localities. Some "ordinary folk" to whom I spoke commended the participatory approach of some RDA efforts. Nonetheless, and to repeat, the CED Division and the RDAs attracting outside companies is presented as a legitimate CED strategy here. This suggests one of many readings of the term *community* economic development: *conventional enterprise **within** a given locale irrespective of the source of capital*. This is not to say that source of capital is irrelevant to the discourse, as will become clearer below.

OPEN TO THE WORLD: OPEN TO EXPLOITATION?

Government is far too differentiated to be characterized as having a single position on development issues. Generally, however, the Canadian polity is committed both publicly and legally to NAFTA and is party to MAI negotiations that will extend free-trade globally. Both federal and provincial governments continue to offer subsidies to externally owned private corporations in the form of infrastructure, grants, and loans.

The impact of external investment on economic *growth*, much less *development*, has been hotly debated.[20] To many theorists (both in the CED community and beyond it), external investment is actually part of the problem of *under*development. Government regional economic development programmes in the 1970s and 1980s—administered by a succession of ever-reorganizing agencies—were oriented to providing relocational incentives to outside investors. They have been widely and openly criticized for squandering public funds on megaprojects that had few positive results.[21] Some led, in fact, to public scandals, such as that of Enterprise Cape Breton (ECB), a federal agency established in 1986 and mandated to offer grants—advertised in the US as "free money"[22]—and loans to industries willing to locate in one of the nation's most stubbornly underdeveloped economic regions. A recent (1997) *Reader's Digest* article revealed, to the nation's public, ECB's report card, which Nova Scotians had long since gleaned piecemeal from local media, revealed that the agency poured millions of public dollars into failed projects; was defrauded by some; had a project success rate of 29 percent; and ultimately spent nearly $110 million to create (1,800) and sustain (750) jobs, without seriously improving the region's unemployment rate.[23]

It is safe to say that development programmes have become more cautious, less generous, and more outcome-driven. It is also clear that more emphasis has been placed on community-based efforts and initiatives. Even as agencies like ECB were subsidizing external enterprisers, "community" was becoming a political buzzword. For example, the Economic Council of Canada, a policy advisory and research organization, published a special report on advocating the CED approach.[24] A Newfoundland Royal Commission had a similar assessment.[25] By the late 1980s, the Canada Employment and Immigration Commission (now part of HRDC, the Human Resources and Development Commission) set up "Community Futures" committees (CFCs) to promote local solutions to economic disparity. Replacing older community initiative programmes, Community Futures was meant to increase and extend local responsibility and control.[26] Given recent experience in reaching outward, as well as the realities of fiscal constraint, Nova Scotia's strategy has stretched downward. By 1994, as noted, RDAs were created to promote community self-help. "The Nova Scotia experience illustrates that people at the local level are the key to making community economic development work," says the lead article in the CED issue of *Nova Scotia: Open to the World*, which goes on to quote then Economic Development and Tourism Minister Richie Mann: "Nova Scotians are recognizing that they have a responsibility to improve their communities, and they are accepting that responsibility."[27] That responsibility is, in effect, downloaded to the RDAs and, through them, to local associations and private citizens. But this does not mean that Nova Scotia, or its regional constituencies, are closed to the outside.

In fact, one case in point offers an interesting model of local/outsider co-operation that helps define the parameters of the role of community in CED. Until 1992, Aerovox Canada, a subsidiary of an American firm, operated an electronics manufacturing plant in Amherst, Cumberland County. Its president, Ben Griffin, discovered that Sola Canada, one of its customers headquartered in Toronto, was also under threat of closure. He and Sola Canada's General Manager Ed Wroebel decided to buy out their firms and establish a new manufacturing company, Ballastronix, which Griffin hoped to see located at Amherst's Aerovox facility, using the town's experienced workforce. (Meanwhile, and to their dismay, the Amherst Area Development Commission and the Cumberland Development Authority, the county's RDA, began to investigate alternative employment opportunities for laid-off workers.) Wroebel put together a consortium of investors but lacked sufficient equity. Griffin is quoted as saying: "the government was willing to help us but they had to have more support on the part of the community."[28] Concretely, that support came in the form of local capital. The RDA found a local investor and enlisted the aid of a local attorney who, with two dozen local businessmen, formed Amherst Community Investments Ltd. The local investors group and the local development commission raised a million dollars to top up

Wroebel's equity pool and make the buy-out a reality. Wroebel, Ballastronix's president, "credits local support, including the equity pool" and an experienced workforce with inducing him to locate his new firm in Amherst rather than (in his words) "the United States or [to] stay in Ontario."[29] By traditional measures, this is a success story. After four years, local investors sold out for 4.3 times their original investment, employment jumped from 72 to a current 200, and the experience is said to have acted as a model for the province's new Equity Tax Credit programme that "hopes to shake money out of mattresses and direct it to community investment funds."[30] Thus, it seems, a significant role for "the community" in CED is provision of private capital for private-sector ventures, even if locals are left in a minority position.

Shaking investment funds out of mattresses for local investment *is* a widely accepted *part of* CED theory and practice. Fr. José Maria Mendizabal (founder of the archetypical Mondragon system of co-operative enterprises) sums up the lesson as a choice: "Savings or Suitcases." By this slogan, the Basque priest exhorted his compatriots to put their savings into the *Caja Laboral Popular* (Credit Union), the major source of Mondragon enterprise investment. The motto "suggests that while money in a National Bank helps create jobs in Madrid, money in their bank (the *Caja*) helps to create jobs in the Basque country."[31] The theme is reiterated in the Northern Ireland investment programme known as "Make Belfast Work," which a Cape Breton activist respondent held up as an inspiration and model. Canadian practitioners and theorists have hailed Quebec's and Saskatchewan's tax equity programme as important local investment incentives. Not only in Cumberland County have Nova Scotian community economic developers lobbied the province to establish such a programme to help keep investment dollars at home. The Nova Scotia programme, which provides a loan guarantee of 20 percent and a 30 percent provincial tax credit to qualified investment, is seen as making local investment safer and more attractive. In Cape Breton, for example, BCA Holdings (a community investment bank) has gained provincial approval to offer the programme to its investors, and there is evidence that the strategy will spread.

While devices to promote local investment are applauded by CED practitioners, attitudes towards outside investment are more complex. CED theorists of various political stripes recognize the tendency of free-market systems to centralize and to chase profits globally at the expense of small communities.[32] In Cape Breton, for example, external ownership of the coal industry moved huge profits out of the region. But as the industry's profitability declined, foreign owners withdrew (in 1966). The Island's foreign-owned steel plant was allowed to deteriorate until it was no longer profitable, and was then taken over by the province (1969), which operated it at a loss (before it was modernized for private sale to outsiders in the mid-1990s). Skepticism about outside ownership is not confined to armchair observers. Many activists not only are aware of local history but also self-consciously pursue local investment for reasons that go beyond access to capital. These reasons can be summarized as the interrelated issues of control and responsibility.

Concern about outside ownership is rooted in an experience which argues that non-locals seek personal profits to the exclusion of concern for community needs. Past government economic-development programmes are criticized not only for carelessness and waste, but also because they did nothing to tether the loose foot of capital.[33] While local loyalty need not preclude profit, integration into the community is seen as curbing the tendency to move on. Commenting upon a joint venture in which both a local private entrepreneur and a community development corporation invested, one observer noted:

> You're going to have a good start for success if you have people like that [the local entrepreneur] own it. If you got someone from

> Ontario that's coming down here to set up a business, that has no interest other than making a quick buck out of the area...See, like what they [outsiders] did was, when the grant money ran out, they went back. A local guy's got to live here. He's not going to run away, is he? He's got a commitment to the area.

MacSween makes the same point regarding "transplant firms," and notes that of those who received ECB sponsorship, firms with all or part Cape Breton ownership were relatively successful.[34]

This is not to say that proponents of local ownership are dogmatic. Some observers applaud Ontario's Magna Corporation for making and maintaining a commitment to its branch plant in North Sydney. This is exceptional. Local CED activists have typically relied on a firmer (financial) tether. BCA Holdings, for example, initiated two large-scale ventures which it could not finance alone. It welcomed capital from firms outside the region, especially since each of these external partners had specific industry expertise. But it organized the projects to ensure that majority equity would be local, and, in one case, BCA itself is the majority shareholder.

The Liberal Tradition

Douglas reserves the term "community economic development" for "*purposeful intervention* on the part of the community or group within the community...It is the economic development *by* the community, *for* the community that distinguishes these initiatives from the development *in* the community, which comes about as a result of the ebb and flow of market forces and occasional government intervention"[35] (emphasis in original). He excludes the industrial development strategies carried out by local governments that were oriented to "selling the community's comparative advantages...[and focused] on capturing a new, and preferably, a large industrial plant."[36] He criticizes the "parade of government programmes," which were common from the 1960s and into the 1980s, that did include community-specific programmes that provoked community response, but did not facilitate "the engagement of the community itself in its own development planning process."[37] He sees the Community Futures Program as an exception.[38]

Fontan likewise sees CED as "efforts to develop local resources from the bottom up,"[39] but, within this, he distinguishes between "liberal" and "progressive" practice. He summarizes the *liberal* approach as entailing initiatives "aimed solely at repairing the economic fabric of the private sector in order to create jobs...Intervention is divided between promotion of local private entrepreneurship and measures to develop the employability of the population."[40] The model assumes that economic growth ("the wealth generated by some") will have a trickle-down effect on the whole community.[41]

It is interesting to examine the Community Futures Program from this perspective. The programme (established 1986) created, in depressed non-metropolitan communities, Community Futures Committees (CFCs) made up of local volunteers nominated by various interest groups. The committees were mandated to assess local development needs, engage in strategic planning, co-ordinate local development, and access other programme components, including significant funding for Business Development Centres (BDCs) and the Self-Employment Assistance or "SEA" programme.[42] In Cape Breton, the CFCs dissolved and the BDCs were transferred to the CED branch of Enterprise Cape Breton Corporation[43] (ECBC, *not* associated with ECB), a federal crown corporation, mandated to promote and help underwrite business development on the Island and a portion of eastern mainland Nova Scotia. The BDCs also administer the SEA programme.

The Canadian government granted each BDC a pool of capital to establish a loan fund to help small- and medium-sized local firms (SMEs) that cannot acquire sufficient credit from conventional banks. In Cape Breton, four BDCs were formed and later consolidated into three. The Northside Economic Development Assistance Corporation (NEDAC), as one of these agencies, will exemplify the model here. It is administered by a board that reviews loan applications and whose members are drawn from the community. The latter is seen as important, because applicants' ability to repay is judged by more than conventional financial measures; assessment of the applicant's character and reputation is crucial. Moreover, the welfare of the community enters consideration, since avoiding redundancy or market-flooding is also a criterion for assessing loan applications. Board members are, also, volunteers who have no personal material interests vested in the agency. Unlike banks, the BDCs have no shareholders to worry about. Loan funds and profits (interest earnings) are returned to the pool for further local investment. Thus, entrepreneurial success breeds further local capacity. The BDCs are also mandated to provide training and business consultation services. NEDAC has been active in this respect.[44]

While the BDCs are more participatory, SEA is bureaucratically run. It aims to help the unemployed to develop private businesses that will provide self-employment—and even, hopefully, eventual employment for others—by offering training and income support to those who are ineligible for EI benefits or whose claims are due to run out during programme participation. Irrespective of degree of local governance, however, both the BDCs and the SEA programme are oriented to traditional, private-sector entrepreneurship. (The YMCA Enterprise Centre is another example of this.) Each, in one or more ways, attempts to add private-sector capacity and extend it to a segment of the population that would otherwise lack entrepreneurial opportunity. In this way, they represent development, rather than mere growth.

"Growth" refers to the generation of wealth, and it is measured merely in terms of the value of transactions that take place using money. The notion of "development," however difficult to specify, includes consideration of how access to material resources is distributed. However, in targeting ventures oriented to private profit, these programmes fall within the range of what can be considered liberal practice. If successful, they will spawn new members of the "bourgeoisie," a class of owners who personally profit from marketing products and services and who do so by buying labour (in wages and salaries).

Some of the practitioners and local observers to whom I spoke approved of development through private enterprise. The facts that small businesses have high failure rates, rarely offer benefits packages, and pay relatively low wages were seen as givens. The private-business model was acceptable, and private business was seen as a boon to local geographical communities because it mitigates against out-migration. Some noted that business operators, like all citizens, should contribute time and effort to community projects. Some said that this qualifies any entrepreneur (including the non-local) as a community economic developer.

The Grassroots

It is perhaps naive to expect governments to be especially innovative. Against the "liberal" form of development, that promotes "no reformist social change," Fontan sets "progressive" practice. Government-based programmes do not tell the whole CED story. Long before governments' conversion to community-based economic development, grassroots initiatives were taking place in Cape Breton. To a real extent, early efforts begat others to form something of a "Family"[45] of organizations. No short discussion can offer a survey that does justice to their diversity. Some have been documented in publications.[46]

Fontan identifies Cape Breton's flagship agency, New Dawn, with *progressive* practice. He also offers checklists of progressive characteristics that are necessarily abstract and thus subject to practical interpretation. They can, still, guide assessments, provoke questions, and generate debate—though they should not lead to mere quibbles about classification. As this chapter strains the boundaries of its allotted space, I regret the impossibility of engaging in a well-rounded exercise of the sort.[47] Let me offer, however, a brief cursive glance through Fontan's framework, not only because discourse is the stock in trade of students and academics but also because provocative issues were raised in the course of my interviews on these matters.

Fontan suggests that progressive practice serves "to integrate economic and social development...[to] improve the community's environment [and] quality of services."[48] At a minimum, I read this to mean that choosing ventures solely for profitability is insufficient. The CED Family has addressed community needs when these were not being met by market forces. For example, the amount and quality of much needed low- to middle-income housing stock in a number of communities was increased. Seniors' housing and services have been extended. Dental clinics were built to help fill the cavernous cavity in that service sector. New uses were found for disused public facilities (e.g., innovative housing at the former Armed Forces radar base and the Reserve Mines "sportsplex" in an abandoned high school).

Consistent with liberal practice, BCA Holdings[49] used local resources "to stimulate and direct private, public, or social-sector investment," but with the *progressive* "aim [of] local control over ownership."[50] For example, it convinced ECBC (a public-sector agency) to provide it a $500,000 loan, by raising a matching amount from local (private) citizen investors. It ploughed some of this into a manufacturing plant (East Coast Ropes) and a radio station (CHER), along with private-sector partners it actively solicited, ensuring that major equity remained local. It entered both these transactions to prevent assets and/or ownership from leaving the community: the American buyers of the rope factory were on the brink of shipping the manufacturing equipment south of the border when BCA stepped in to help local citizens protest the move and to organize a buy-out. CHER was in receivership, and a Montreal company was interested in its purchase when BCA formed a partnership with Maritime Broadcasting and successfully bid for it.

A further criterion of progressive practice seems both crucial and difficult to define operationally: namely, "a priority is accorded to alternative, non-traditional economic forms (cooperatives, alternative businesses, community enterprises, self-management, non-profit organizations)."[51] In essence, the degree to which any model can be called non-traditional, and the degree to which any actual CED innovates with socio-economic forms, are matters of interpretation. Insofar as the Cape Breton CED Family is a group of not-for-profit organizations administered by boards of local volunteers, they (like the BDCs) can be called at least minimally non-traditional. But they invest in, and sometimes operate, for-profit businesses that are run like private-sector firms. They are, in a sense, hybrids. BCA is particularly so. It offers, to the public, preferred shares in some of its enterprises and in its subsidiary BCA Venture Capital. It also engages in partnerships with private entrepreneurs who make personal profits. BCA also sells the equivalent of GICs, and while investors profit from their capital, any additional earnings from its ventures are under collective control of the not-for-profit organization.

One factor that distinguishes the "Family" (from what may be considered left-liberal agencies like the BDCs) is that some profits can be routinely applied to non-profit service activities (such as New Dawn's Volunteer Resource Centre). New Dawn, like other Family members, is less subject to pressures to satisfy private partners or individual investors, because it independently operates a collection of mutually sustaining companies. Though its governors insist that they be run like any business, its varied enterprises can temporarily underwrite one another and compensate for those that are less successful in market terms but are serving community needs. Thus, for example, it ran a money-losing guest home for years, whereas a private firm would surely have long before abandoned it. (In fact, New Dawn bought it to rescue it from closure.)

Some leaders of the CED Family find fault with co-operatives (at least, those more established ones that exist at the retail and consumer level) for being too bureaucratic, remote and narrowly focused. Some sentiment is dubious of worker co-ops, as well, because they are insufficiently communitarian; rather, workers are suspected as being an "interest group" like any other, such as capitalist investors. To my knowledge, none of the Family's businesses offers employees profit-sharing plans. Some spokespersons that I interviewed see unions as an institution of the past, inappropriate to the construction of CED institutions *qua* 21st-century organizations. Indeed, the Family has engaged in only one short-term abortive experiment with the worker co-op form. Likewise, I can see no evidence of employee self-management in the Family's organizations. The companies are managed conventionally; none has schooled its employees for board appointments or to act as informed advocates of a CED movement.

Not surprisingly, no one to whom I spoke (inside or outside the Family) failed to recognize that industrial Cape Breton is better off because of these and the many other efforts of this Family of CED organizations. Ironically, perhaps, some of the interviewed observers expected CED organizations (but not private enterprises) to be "representative of and accountable to their community," as progressive practices are meant to be,[52] and they criticized the local groups for falling short of this standard. There are two common concerns about the way governance structures are constituted within the Family. First, board appointment procedures not open enough to broad community input. Second, business people and relatively well-educated residents are over-represented among governors. These practices may lead to the evolution of a new, local, administrative elite, who act as patrons of lesser folk and function as caretakers rather than as instruments of empowerment of the marginalized.[53] These criticisms deserve far more careful analysis than can be provided here. But they need mention, if only to suggest that more work in the community is required if the Family is to enlist broad public support, create a universal sense of community ownership, and develop a desired communitarian ethic.

SPECTRUM AND PRISM

In general, grassroots practice seems more progressive than government initiatives have been to date. The foregoing survey suggests that CED action is better described as a spectrum than a typology. Fontan offers us two categories, but real-life examples follow a gradient, and one which should perhaps be extended to a "radical" far end. When Greg MacLeod[54] tells us that nothing in North America is comparable to the Mondragon miracle, he speaks of its asset base, comprehensiveness, integration, and global competitiveness. But Mondragon is also unusually innovative in its degree of worker participation in governance and profit-sharing. Some of those who spoke to me would, I think, argue that even Mondragon does not go far enough in these respects, while others would argue that the demands for expertise and efficiency put Mondragon on the leading edge of what is possible. Likewise, there are those who argue that the most truly disempowered must be more directly involved and centrally placed in the practice of CED. Others would respond that the challenges of our contemporary complex economy require specialized, advanced knowledge, which the most marginalized are unlikely to have. Perhaps the crisis is too great to permit an expansion of the range of reasonable experimentation.

In the simple economies that anthropologists traditionally studied, ordinary people were radically independent, having no public or private sector on whom to rely, and having ready access to the means of directly making a living for themselves. The world has changed; few are so empowered. Not too long ago, Prime Minister Chrétien was widely cited in the media when he asserted that it is not the government's responsibility to create employment, but that that role belongs, rather, to the private sector. But today's ascendant neoconservativism acknowledges that the proper goal of the private sector is profit, not employment creation. Indeed, global competition creates pressure for corporate downsizing and for capital investment in new labour-saving technologies. These messages have reached the public. The notion that the days of government largesse are over has become widespread. Rhetoric about the evils of "dependency" is epidemic. If neither the public-sector nor major private-sector players, as we have traditionally defined them, can provide a means of livelihood to the majority of the population, what remains? This is the context in which CED finds its significance. Today's conventional wisdom is this: we have to learn to help ourselves. "We" can mean the individuals who create self-employment and, it can mean the groups that seek more communal localized entrepreneurship. How we help ourselves, in the face of massive "restructuring," is far from clear. But we can hope that experimentation, as well as analysis and debate, will continue.

ENDNOTES

1. See, for example, Jean-Marc Fontan. *A Critical Review of Canadian, American, & European Community Economic Development*

Literature, Vancouver: CCE/Westcoast Publications, 1993; and Jack Quarter, *Canada's Social Economy: Co-operatives, Non-profits, and Other Community Enterprises,* Toronto: James Lorimer & Company, 1992.

2. See David J.A Douglas, ed., *Community Economic Development in Canada,* Vol. 2, Toronto: McGraw-Hill Ryerson, 1995; or Eric Shragge, ed., *Community Economic Development: In Search of Empowerment,* 2nd ed., Montréal: Black Rose Books, 1997.

3. Gertrude Anne MacIntyre, *Active Partners: Education and Local Development.* Sydney: University College of Cape Breton Press, 1995.

4. Constance P. deRoche, *The Village, The Vertex: Adaptation to Regionalism and Development in a Complex Society.* Occasional Papers in Anthropology, 12, Halifax: Department of Anthropology, St. Mary's University, 1985; Constance P. deRoche and John E. deRoche, eds., *"A Rock in a Stream: Living with the Political Economy of Underdevelopment in Cape Breton,* Research and Policy Papers 7. St. John's: Institute of Social and Economic Research, Memorial University of Newfoundland, 1987.

5. Some of the background research on which this chapter is based was sponsored by a small grant from the University's Research Evaluation Committee. I was also granted a sabbatical leave (1997-98) by the financially strapped University College of Cape Breton. It allowed me time to read and to conduct a number of in-depth interviews both in and beyond Cape Breton. I am grateful for this support and also for the generosity of those who took the time to talk to me.

6. None of these is easy to summarize, but I can very briefly sketch out some issues here. *Community,* for example, can be defined as an area-based collectivity or one based on commonality of status, interest, and identity. At least among anthropologists, there is no consensus on what constitutes *economics.* One school agrees essentially with economists: it is the study of self-interested maximizing behaviour, making choices under conditions of scarcity (economizing). Another group insists this is culturally biased and ideological; they prefer to focus on behaviour that serves a wide range of needs and that can be quite altruistic in certain sociocultural contexts. *Development* is perhaps hardest to define. Since the late 1970s, practitioners and analysts have become impatient with traditional aggregate measures such as Gross National Product that focus on money value. *Development* (as opposed to mere growth) has come to be seen in terms of distributive and quality-of-life issues.

7. *Nova Scotia: Open to the World* (Halifax: Atlantic Progress Publishers, July 1997), p. 1.

8. Ibid.

9. Ibid. p. 10.

10. Ibid. p. 28.

11. Ibid. p. 23.

12. Ibid. p. 14.

13. Ibid. p. 28.

14. Ibid. p. 20.

15. Ibid. p. 23.

16. Ibid. p. 28.

17. Ibid. p. 14.

18. Ibid.

19. David J.A. Douglas, "Community Economic Development in Canada: Issues, Scope, and Definitions and Directions," in *Community Economic Development in Canada*, Vol. 1., edited by David J.A. Douglas. Toronto: McGraw-Hill Ryerson, 1994a, p. 25.

20. There is a vast scholarly literature on this topic. Atlantic Canadian social scientists and historians have generated—largely in the heyday of "dependency theory"—a critical analysis of external ownership that shifted capital, corporate headquarters, and profits to Central Canada and beyond. A detailed discussion is contained in Ralph Matthews, *The Creation of Regional Dependency*, Toronto: University of Toronto Press, 1983. For a more brief and recent survey see Peter Sinclair, "Underdevelopment and Regional Inequality." Pp. 358-376 in *Social Issues and Contradictions in Canadian Society*, edited by B. Singh Bolaria. Toronto: Harcourt Brace Jovanovich, Canada, 1991. The issue is also central in debates about international development; for a recent review see Ted C. Lewellen, *Dependency and Development: An Introduction to the Third World*. Westport, CT: Bergin & Garvey, 1995. For a recent general critique of the impact of the global economy, see Jerry Mander and Edward Goldsmith, eds. *The Case Against the Global Economy*. San Francisco: Sierra Club Books, 1996. It contains an especially relevant section, "Steps Toward Relocalization."

21. MacIntyre; also J. Rankin MacSween. *The Values Underlying a Community Development Corporation.* Ph.D. (Dissertation, Department of Education, University of Toronto, 1994).

22. MacSween, p. 73.

23. Doug Small, "Fresh Start for Cape Breton," in *Reader's Digest,* February 1997, p. 62.

24. Tim O'Neil, *From the Bottom Up: The Community Economic Development Approach.* Ottawa: Economic Council of Canada, 1990.

25. Douglas House, *Building on our Strengths: The Report of the Royal Commission on Employment and Unemployment.* St. John's: The Queen's Printer, 1986.

26. For more detail and other sources, see Greg MacLeod, *The Concept in Operation,* Sydney: Tompkins Institute, University College of Cape Breton, 1991a; and David J.A. Douglas, ed. "Context and Conditions of Community Economic Development in Canada: Governmental Institutional Responses." Pp. 65-118 in *Community Economic Development in Canada*, Vol. 1, edited by David J.A. Douglas. Toronto: McGraw-Hill Ryerson, 1994b.

27. Joey Fitzpatrick, "Taking Charge," in *Nova Scotia Open to the World,* July 1997, p. 4.

28. Allan Lynch, "As Good as Gold," in *Nova Scotia Open to the World,* July 1997, p. 12.

29. Ibid.

30. Ibid.

31. Greg MacLeod, *From Mondragon to America: Experiments in Community Economic Development.* Sydney: University College of Cape Breton Press, 1997, p. 22.

32. Christopher Bryant,"The Locational Dynamics of Community Economic Development," pp. 203-236 in *Community Economic Development in Canada*, Vol. 1, edited by David J.A. Douglas, Toronto: McGraw-Hill Ryerson, 1994; Brett Fairbairn, et al., eds., *Co-operatives & Community Development: Economics in Social Perspective,* Saskatoon: Centre for the Study of Co-operatives, University of Saskatchewan, 1995; Christopher Gunn and Hazel Dayton Gunn, *Reclaiming Capital: Democratic Initiative and Community Development,* Ithaca: Cornell University Press, 1991; Mander and Goldsmith,

op. cit.; Marcia Nozick, *No Place Like Home: Building Sustainable Communities.* Ottawa: Canadian Council on Social Development, 1992.

33. MacLeod, *op. cit.*, 1991a, p. 9; MacSween, *op. cit.*, p. 101.

34. MacSween, *op. cit.,* pp. 77, 101.

35. David J.A. Douglas, *op. cit.,* 1994a, p. 22.

36. Ibid. p. 25.

37. Ibid.

38. Ibid.

39. Fontan, *op.cit.,* p. 3.

40. Ibid. pp. 6, 8.

41. Ibid. p. 6.

42. David J.A. Douglas, *Community Economic Development and You,* Ottawa: Employment and Immigration Canada, 1992; Douglas, *op.cit.*, 1994b, esp. p. 95; Fontan, *op., cit.*, pp. 22-23.

43. Among its many functions, ECBC offers two loan programmes to small and medium sized businesses that it deems beneficial to the community, especially with respect to job creation. The programmes are administered bureaucratically; they are non-participatory. Thus they can be seen as "local development" rather than as CED programmes, in Douglas' usage *(op. cit.,* 1994a, p. 22ff). The programmes do not, in fact, describe themselves as CED.

44. This is very briefly summarized in Constance P. deRoche, comp. *Entrepreneurial Resource Guide.* Sydney: Community Economic Development Institute, 1998 (forthcoming).

45. For the sake of convenience I will use this word "Family" to refer to a cluster of organizations whose origins and inspiration are related. These include BCA, New Dawn, New Deal, Tompkins Development, and Umbrella Development Group. This cluster does not exhaust the list of community-based, non-governmental efforts, such as those of the Cape Breton Women's Community Development Network, as well as the work being done by local affiliates of national and international non-governmental organizations like the Calmeadow Foundation (see deRoche, *op. cit.,* 1998). Consideration of these must, unfortunately, await a later opportunity.

46. For more information, see Greg MacLeod, *New Age Business,* Ottawa: The Canadian Council on Social Development, 1986; Greg MacLeod, *New Dawn Enterprises,* Sydney: Tompkins Institute, University College of Cape Breton, 1991b; MacLeod, *op. cit.,* 1997; and MacSween, *op. cit.,* as well as "New Dawn Enterprises Ltd.: A Community Economic Development Experiment," pp. 182-191 in *Community Economic Development: In Search of Empowerment,* 2nd ed., edited by Eric Shragge. Montréal: Black Rose Books, 1997. For bare descriptions of some that have not otherwise been memorialized in print, see deRoche, *op. cit.,* 1998.

47. MacSween, *op. cit.,* 1994 devotes a dissertation to analyzing New Dawn and attends to the issue both implicitly throughout and more specifically on pp. 169-183.

48. Fontan, *op. cit.,* p. 5.

49. BCA Holdings Ltd. is more structurally and functionally complex than is revealed here. For a bird's eye view, see deRoche, *op. cit.,* 1998. A videotape description of the organization has been produced; a booklet on it (part of the Community Business Series) by Greg MacLeod, is forthcoming. They are distributed by New View Productions Ltd. P. O. Box 1201, Sydney, N.S. B1P 6J9.

50. Fontan, *op. cit.,* pp. 7, 8.

51. Ibid. p. 8.

52. Ibid.

53. In fact, some social scientists argue that real power rests in the hands of those who manage, not necessarily those who own, capital.

54. MacLeod, *op. cit.,* 1997.

An Ear to the Ground: Grassroots Concerns About Employment and Economic Development
Angus MacIntyre

Introduction

In March 1995, I returned to Cape Breton Island after spending ten years in northern Manitoba and northern Ontario working in the field of community-based economic development at the municipal level. As I reintegrated myself into community life in Cape Breton, I became interested in what appeared to be a prevailing attitude among Cape Bretoners—that somehow if someone would only give them a job, their problems (and by extension Cape Breton's problems) would be solved. My hunch was that people's attitudes about economic development and job creation are influenced by their perception of how these issues impact upon them personally. I also suspected that some people perceived themselves as having little influence or control over local economic conditions and that this belief would influence their attitude about local development and employment.

The idea that jobs would be the answer also seemed to prevail among a number of political and community leaders, as well as among professionals assigned to work on economic development. My experience over the years suggested to me that a job, just any job, was not the answer to economic underdevelopment in Cape Breton.

I decided that I would use every opportunity to question the attitudes and opinions held by local people regarding the important topics of economic development and employment so that I might obtain a clearer picture of these issues. It is my nature to try to encourage dialogue, and my questions invariably stimulated discussion and questioning. These discussions were widespread, involving friends, acquaintances and strangers, as well as officials and leaders whom I encountered in my daily activities. I quickly learned that these questions were of great interest to the people with whom I spoke, or, more importantly, to whom I listened. For the most part, these were ordinary people, often referred to collectively as "the grassroots."

Since 1995, I have recorded the results of conversations with approximately 150 people in more than a dozen Cape Breton Island communities. The communities included Whycocomagh, Waycobah, Waymatcook, Scotsville, Margaree Harbour, Margaree Forks, Cheticamp, Pleasant Bay, Bay St. Lawrence, Ingonish, Baddeck, Inverness, Mabou, Port Hood, St. Peters, and Big Pond, all centres where I was either working or visiting friends, relatives and colleagues. I have recorded discussions with a smaller number of people from Port Hawkesbury, Sydney Mines, Glace Bay, and Louisbourg, communities that are experiencing serious economic difficulties. The rationale for my activity was my interest in learning what people thought about local economic conditions and what, if anything, they were prepared to do about these conditions. My questioning was never intended to provide answers to the economic or social ills of Cape Bretoners. At the time I had no intent to publish what I was learning in the process. Only after the fact did I realize that it might be useful to share the insights I had gained.

I undertook my research whenever I was presented with the opportunity to dialogue informally with grassroots people. The interviews occurred when I was in a village or town for social or cultural gatherings (weddings, social visits, funerals and cultural events, among others), or for recreation (for instance, playing golf). My context was always a natural one—that is, I did not try to transform a real-life situation into an artificial research setting. Neither did I take on the formal identity of researcher or outside expert. Rather, I wanted to listen, as one ordinary person among other ordinary people.

METHODOLOGY

In this task, I was influenced by Michael Patton's work on qualitative methodology.[1] Patton has written three important publications dealing with the use of qualitative surveys and questionnaires as a method of behavioural science research. His premise is that qualitative techniques, such as interviewing people without a formalized survey, questionnaire, or formal interview time and place, are valid methods of inquiry. He also believes that the results have as much credibility (and in some cases more so) than the traditional methods of social science research.

After listening to people talk about jobs or the lack of jobs over a period of six months, I found certain themes recurring regularly in our conversations. At this point, I decided to develop a series of questions to encourage people to talk freely about their attitudes and feelings about economic development and the problem of unemployment. I used these questions as a guideline when talking with people throughout Cape Breton. This approach allowed the person being heard to control the flow of the conversation. Probing responses to their statements invariably led to a deeper exploration of the issue. I did not record or make notes at the time of the conversations, but I did make notes afterwards.

An informal interview is, by definition, interactive. Since the responses themselves influence the course of discussion, the exchange cannot be rigidly structured, nor can all questions be preordained. I was careful to ensure that certain pivotal concerns were raised with all respondents. I asked a variety of questions. One set focused on employment preferences; a second set centred on a number of economic development issues. I also asked about people's general economic aspirations for their families and community. These queries and people's responses to them are discussed in more detail in separate subsections below.

After approximately a year and a half of conducting these informal interviews, patterns began to emerge in the responses. I began to gain insight into how people really felt about these important issues.

LOCAL ATTITUDES ON EMPLOYMENT PREFERENCES

As the research proceeded, a general pattern of response emerged. The following composite portrait reflects a typical dialogue about employment preferences:

Question: Hi there. What's happening?

Response: Oh, nothing, nothing at all.

Question: Why not?

Response: There's no work. I haven't worked in months/years.

Question: There's not much going on here, eh?

Response: No, not since I got laid off from....

Question: I assume if you had a job, it would solve all of your problems?

Response: Yeah, it sure would. If I only had a job, all of my problems would be over.

Question: Let's assume for a minute that you have a job. What else would you need to be content or happy?

Response: Nothing really. I would be satisfied with a job.

Question: Would it matter, what kind of a job?

Response: No, not really, as long as it's work.

Question: So a job paying minimum wages would be okay with you?

Response: Well, heck, no. It would have to pay enough to provide a decent living for me and....

Question: Oh! So if you had a job that paid a reasonable wage, what else would you want the job to do for you if you had a choice?

Response: Nothing. A good paying job would satisfy me.

Question: So given a choice, it wouldn't matter to you if you were slinging hamburgers at McDonalds or working in a factory doing routine work?

Response: Oh yeah, well given a choice, I would like to do something useful, something I am interested in.

Question: So if you had a job, that paid well, and it was interesting work, you would be perfectly happy?

Response: Absolutely.

Question: You wouldn't need or want anything else?

Response: No, absolutely not.

Question: And if you had this perfect job, how long would you like to see it last?

Response: Well, indefinitely of course. There is nothing worse than these temporary, make work projects. They teach you bad work habits and never lead anywhere. Six months later you're back where you started.

Question: So if you had a job, a well paying, meaningful, permanent job, your problems would be solved and you would be happy?

Response: Well, the obvious answer should be "yes," but I hesitate to say that because I know you are going to come up with another question that is going to make me think about my answer, right?

Question: You've got that right. I've been found out. Only now you have reversed the tables and YOU are starting to ask the questions.

These discussions often began by people complaining about the lack of jobs or job opportunities on Cape Breton Island.

Although ordinary people seem merely to want any kind of job, when they are invited to elaborate their feelings, they reveal that they want more: it is long-term, meaningful work that they want.

Defining Economic Development

I began by asking people what they thought economic development is all about. These discussions demonstrated similar results to those on employment in that they often began by complaining about someone "out there" not bringing "jobs" to their community.

These informal interviews illustrated to me that most people interpreted economic development as being about recruiting new industry to the region. In almost every instance, they thought of these new industries as factories or manufacturing plants of some kind. They did not relate the type of industry to any of Cape Breton's natural resources, except in a few instances where individuals expressed the hope for a small fish plant. As one person who had done some thinking about the subject of job creation expressed it, "From what I have been reading, I know we shouldn't be chasing smokestacks. But it would be nice to get the factory, probably a warehouse with computers in it, without the smokestack. I guess that's what this new global economy is all about."

Most people didn't talk about the need to help existing businesses and industries or the desirability of creating new local business. A considerable number felt that any attempt by a local person to "make it" in the business world would be met with jealousy and suspicion, rather than support and encouragement. Different people made the point using exactly the same words: "We are our own worst enemy."

Responsibility For Economic Development

I often followed up by asking people who should be responsible for economic development. More than half of those with whom I talked did not know who was currently responsible for economic development, nor did they have an opinion on who should be. Many of those who did have an opinion said their local politician was responsible, while others said "government" was responsible. None I talked with saw themselves as having primary responsibility to do anything about the economic conditions of their community or region.

Most were unfamiliar with the various agencies having a mandate to promote economic development in their community or region. Few could offer details about the kinds of programmes or services available in the region to help people start their own businesses or to create jobs. Only three individuals with whom I spoke had first-hand experience with any of the agencies directly responsible for economic development, and those experiences had not been positive ones.

In the first case, a couple wanted to experiment with a new agricultural product. They told me that they were referred from one agency to another—local, regional and provincial. In their estimation, they were given no help, information or encouragement. They were told over and over again that their idea did not make sense and would never work. These same people have now operated their business successfully for a year and are currently exporting their product internationally. As one of them said, "We have been successful at doing this *in spite of* all the agencies out there who are supposed to help, not *because of* them."

The second case differs somewhat. The individual was successful in plugging into a government programme designed to help new businesses get started. The problem in this situation, however, was the apparent lack of understanding and support he received from those in agencies that were supposed to help. He told me that he was often referred from one employee to another and from one agency to another, resulting in months to get an answer to a simple question. He reported that the business counseling he received consisted of the government employee telling him what he did or did not need and under what conditions he would receive help. When these conditions did not meet the needs of his business, he reported that the attitude of those who were supposed to assist him was, "Take it or leave it. You are getting it for nothing anyway." He felt that the agency staff viewed him as ungrateful when he questioned the conditions under which he could receive help. The individual in question finally refused the financial help that he was entitled to rather than change his business plan in order to meet the government's criteria. He now has a successful business in Cape Breton and is exporting his product to the United States.

Public Involvement In Economic Development

I asked people if they had ever been involved in discussions about the future economic development of their communities or region. A few had heard of local public meetings where economic development was a topic but had not taken any personal interest in attending those meetings. Most people thought that having a meeting on the subject was a good idea. Many felt they couldn't understand what makes an economy tick or how they might be involved in economic activity. They felt that economic development and job creation should be left to the experts, whom they identified as government staff, university teachers, business leaders, and consultants as the experts. Most felt they had nothing of value to offer. Only a few said that if they were approached to help, they would volunteer their time to assist with problem-solving related to this issue.

Funding Of Economic Development

When I asked the question, "Who should fund economic development?" almost unanimously people said that the greatest responsibility for funding economic development belongs to the federal government, followed closely by the provincial government. A number of people stated that local government should not be funding economic development because they feared this would lead to higher local taxes. They saw the job of the local politician as being to fight for grants from the provincial and federal government, not to devote scarce local resources to economic development, which they thought was beyond local influence or control.

No one thought private industry could be expected to be responsible for creating jobs. Industry was seen to be in the business of making a profit; therefore, employing as few people as possible would be their goal. Many cited banking institutions as the epitome of corporate concern for profits.

Local people could not identify any major corporation which concerned itself with social issues or economic development in their area. Several small local firms, however, were identified as being concerned with local conditions, as being generous when asked to support a local cause, providing funds, material goods or volunteers. They were seen as having a commitment to the health of the local community.

The Economic Future – Discouragement and Hope

When I asked whether they thought economic conditions would improve in the foreseeable future (that is, by the year 2000), most said no, that they believed that the situation would worsen in the immediate future. They could not envision a day when Cape Breton would achieve a ten percent unemployment rate or less. No one I spoke to believed the unemployment figures reported in the media. Many thought the real rate of unemployment was two or three times the figures now being used by the experts.

Nearly all of those I talked with said they would not discourage their friends from leaving the Island, nor would they encourage their friends and relatives who had already moved away to return, to Cape Breton, except to retire. Almost everyone had a story about at least one friend or relative who had recently left Cape Breton. Within a ten-mile stretch of road, one individual identified eight families who had moved away in the previous few months.

In these conversations, it became obvious that people feel angry, powerless, and discouraged about Cape Breton's economic prospects for the near future. They see local economic problems as deriving from "those government bean counters who make decisions about our communities and our lives, which they know nothing about." Within these negative expressions, however, I was able to find a spark of hope. It came at a moment of insight, when I realized what lay beneath the complaints and criticisms I had heard. People's complaints were, after all, focused on conditions about which they felt very strongly. Though they saw harm being done to them and felt that solutions were beyond their control, they cared deeply about their own situations and about their communities. When questions were framed in a manner that gave them a chance to imagine things being better, they quickly began to describe what could be done. They talked about highways, water and sewer systems, education, and health care as areas where great savings could be realized if the government consulted with local communities before decisions were made. Tourism was often cited as an area where the existing strategy could be improved. The feeling was that if improvements in signage, roads, scenic lookouts, picnic facilities, and waterfront developments were made in consultation with the local people as the first concern, then the tourists would come in larger numbers, not because of these improvements but because they wanted to experience the local way of life. The essence of the responses I got wherever I went was this: What people want for their communities is sustainable development, leading to independence and self-reliance.

Family and Community

I asked, "Given a meaningful choice, what would you want for your family and your community?" This lead question opened the way for interactive interviews, like those about employment preferences noted above. While the context of the conversation was economic development, the response was often much broader than the economy or jobs. People talked about the importance of maintaining local schools, because schools are the heart of the community. Their arguments with local school boards had as much to do with the quality of education and whether or not it was preparing their children for the world they would live in, as it did with economies of scale, whether bigger is better, or whether more is better or even necessary.

They spoke about the importance of music and dance, not in economic terms, but for the maintenance of local values and culture. Although more and more economists are increasingly identifying the economic impact that cultural activities have on a community, many of the individuals I talked with felt that these activities had an intrinsic value—and that it was not right to put a strictly economic value on them. The Celtic Colours International Festival, held in October 1997 throughout Cape Breton Island, for instance, evoked positive comment, not because it was an economic success, or because it extended the tourist season, but because it gave local communities another opportunity to come together and celebrate their spirit, which many feel is still alive and well. People told me that part of the Cape Breton tradition is its strong history of self-reliance and independence, something that several felt was gradually being eroded. Most people I talked with didn't want progress at any price. They wanted to keep many of their traditional values, but they also recognized that to do so, they also had to sustain their community's economic well-being. Still, how to do this was a question most people looked to government to answer.

Conclusions and Recommendations

The most important initiative that can be undertaken by officials who are responsible for economic development on Cape Breton Island is this: developing and implementing a strategic plan for regional or community development that is *acceptable to, and owned by, the community.* It should be at the forefront of their agenda. Such officials have the difficult, challenging task of obtaining and preserving community support for their efforts. However, local leaders (business, religious and elected), professional economic developers and consultants who prepare strategic economic development plans for an area often discover that their efforts to promote economic development are criticized and opposed by those they are attempting to assist. To successfully participate with local people in creating sustainable communities, it is imperative that local leaders and economic development workers earn the support of local people.

An important first step in this process is for those leaders to understand what the average local person *knows* and *feels* about economic development in his or her own area. They must understand what local people see as their future, and how they feel economic development will help them meet their goals and objectives. And they must include women in this dialogue, since women created more than half of the successful small businesses in Canada in recent years.

Formal leaders and senior administrators will not learn what grassroots people are thinking by going out into communities to *talk at*, or even *to talk to* the people they represent. It will only come about if formal leaders and civil servants learn how *to ask*, and how *to listen* to the people.

My exploration of this subject only uncovers the tip of the iceberg. We need more research. The questions we have to ask ourselves are: Who should conduct such research? Should it be left to the experts, the academics, or the government? Who has a vested interest in seeing that this research is carried out? I advocate participatory research, a method which would involve Cape Breton communities in helping to formulate questions of a social, economic, cultural, spiritual, educational and political nature that are of concern to them. If such questions are designed to link grassroots aspirations to sustainable economic activity, that would sustain not only body and soul, but also the spirit of the people, then individuals, organizations and entire communities would, I believe, come alive in the pursuit of a better life.

On the basis of my experience as a researcher and practitioner, I am convinced that various stakeholders–elected officials, business leaders, religious leaders, community organizations and groups, from fire departments to women's groups to multicultural, agricultural, fisheries, recreational and social groups—would if properly approached, volunteer to become involved in such a process. What has been lacking is the leadership to make it happen. Institutions need to link up and reach out to interested individuals and organizations on the Island, in collaborative inquiry. By doing so, they would be creating a true community initiative. If they do, we may just be able to identify the important questions to ask ourselves to act upon the challenges of the future.

An earlier version of this chapter appeared in the publication of KANATA INSTITUTE FOR EXPERIENTIAL LEARNING AND COLLABORATIVE RESEARCH, 1997.

Reprinted by permission.

ENDNOTES

1. Michael Quinn Patton. *Qualitative Evaluation Methods.* Beverly Hills, CA.: Sage Publications, 1980.

    -----*Practical Evaluation.* Beverly Hills, CA: Sage Publications, 1982.

    -----*Utilization Focused Evaluation.* Beverly Hills, CA.: Sage Publications, 1986.

13

MARGINALITY, LIMINALITY AND LOCAL DEVELOPMENT
JIM LOTZ

The current enthusiasm for community economic development will continue to accelerate as the mainstream economy proves increasingly unable to generate enough jobs in advanced industrial nations. In the developing nations and the former communist countries, community-based development of all kinds offers an alternative to domination of the economy by the rich and powerful who practice the most extreme forms of exploitive, uncaring and unbridled capitalism. As gaps widen between rich and poor, the centre and the edges of society, the comfortable past and the uncertain future, community economic development begins to appeal to governments concerned with creating employment for those on the margins of society and in depressed regions. Only too often, community economic development is invoked by governments when all other ways of stimulating the economy have failed.

Is community economic development a forlorn hope, a last gasp of official agencies whose previous policies and plans have failed to create a better life for those whose fate they have made themselves responsible? Or is it a new harbinger, a promising way of tackling local development in ways that will give residents more control over their own destinies and by doing so create a new economic order?

In the 1960s, community development was espoused as a way of bringing the outsiders in Canadian society into fuller participation in the life of the nation. In 1966, Prime Minister Lester Pearson claimed that:

> As a philosophy and a method, community development offers a way of involving people more fully in the life of their communities. It generates scope and initiatives which enable people to participate creatively in the economic, social and cultural life of a nation. It provides, above all, a basis for a more profound understanding and effective use of democratic processes. These are the essential elements of Canada's social policy.[1]

In the 1960s, it seemed as if optimism and good intentions would solve all Canada's social problems. In those days, the community development movement attracted a diversity of people bent on improving the lives of others through interventions by government agencies. The results of these interventions ranged from small improvements to changes that rendered communities more fragmented and powerless than they had been before community development was invoked as a panacea.[2]

The community economic development movement emerged as depressions hit Canada in the 1980s, and the traditional ways of dealing with their aftermaths proved less and less effective. In particular, efforts at regional development and reliance on such approaches as growth centres, the creation of industrial parks, megaprojects and high-tech failed to generate new ventures and new jobs. In its 1990 statement, *From the Bottom Up: the Community Economic Development Approach*, the Economic Council of Canada noted:

> ...Canada's unemployment problem is, in part, a problem of smaller and more remote com-

munities whose resource base is depleted or diminished by weak prices. If they are to survive and to provide economic opportunities for their citizens, these communities need to mobilize new resources, to diversify their economic base. But many of them lack the skills needed for this diversification. Governments have tried to change the situation but the disparities and the stagnation remain. As a result, top-down, bureaucracy-driven plans for regional development have fallen into disrepute and policymakers know they need to consider new approaches. One of the new approaches is community-based economic development.[3]

This rather simplistic statement ignores the complex ways in which unemployment is generated in advanced industrial economies struggling to cope with structural changes and global competition. Weak prices for resources is only one factor in creating unemployment in small and remote communities. In some places, such as Schefferville in Québec, the resource has simply been depleted; no amount of diversification in this remote northern community will make it the prosperous place it once was when the iron mines were in full production. And the claim that community-based economic development is a "new approach" ignores the history of co-operatives and credit unions in Canada.

The Economic Council of Canada commissioned a number of case studies on community economic development. Subsumed under the term is a curious collection of local initiatives. In many cases, the community economic development ventures originated through the efforts of a single individual who helped local people focus their attention on their situation and move into action. In northern Saskatchewan, a Vietnam War veteran in search of peace and quiet helped an

Indian band to reorganize its business ventures and enter into joint ventures with non-aboriginal companies in mutually beneficial ways.[4] HRDA in Halifax originated through the vision and efforts of a perceptive local government official who recognized that people on Social Assistance wanted real jobs and not just "workfare."[5] On Price Edward Island, an individual with a business background brought new life to a regional development venture.[6] A collective effort by members of a community came about when a crisis hit Eagle River on the North Shore of Labrador: a bank pulled out of the town and the whole community came together to establish a local credit union,[7] the bank manager stayed in the community to help its birth, and a *caisse populaire* in a nearby Québec community provided advice and guidance.

Using community economic development simply as yet another technique or tool for helping poor and marginalized people and regions ignores some ethical and moral dimensions of social change. Both Karl Marx and Adam Smith reduced humans to "factors of production." Now people wish to see themselves as participants in controlling and directing their own lives. They no longer wish to be seen as extensions of machines, as consumers of goods, as victims or bystanders in ventures designed and implemented without their involvement.

Matthews, in his study of regional development, cites Habermas on the crisis of legitimization that occurs when a political system is unable to accomplish the economic goals it sets for itself:

> A kind of legitimation crisis is occurring today is Canadian regional development....Those for who plans are being made increasingly resist measures which often seem designed to undercut their local culture and way of life. On the one hand, the planners themselves seem to be going through an identity crisis of their own, in

which they question their own legitimacy and ability to make plans....A general feeling of helplessness appears to have permeated regional planning throughout the country...[8]

A recent volume of essays showed the differing responses to community development in Canada. In New Brunswick and Prince Edward Island, initial enthusiasm for community-based development faded when local organizations began to question the wisdom and actions of government agencies intervening in their lives.[9] Government responded by cutting the funding of local grassroots ventures, claiming that they had achieved their goals and were no longer needed. In Québec, on the other hand, the Parti Québecois has shown wild enthusiasm for community-based development. But its critics claim that the government is using community economic development as an inexpensive way of providing services to poor people and poor communities, and generating jobs by providing a few extra dollars a week to people who move off the welfare rolls and go to work for community agencies. There is also considerable tension in Quebec between professionals and amateurs in community development.[10]

Nova Scotia has sought to follow a middle course in community economic development, seeing the processes involved in it as complementing traditional methods of creating jobs and new business ventures. The Liberal government came to power in 1993 on a platform of involving Nova Scotians in determining their economic and social destinies. This promise proved difficult to keep as the government embarked on efforts to decentralize the school and health systems and to stimulate community economic development. Two individuals played a key role in putting into place what was needed to give local people more control over their own economic destinies. Community development is often presented as a form of spontaneous combustion that suddenly burst into flame in a community through the collective efforts of its members. In fact, it always relies on one or two gifted, skilled and experienced individuals to encourage the processes necessary to begin the difficult task of creating organizations that can actually undertake community-based development, rather than just talking about it. In Nova Scotia in the mid-1990s, an "insider" who had worked with a regional development agency and was respected by politicians and senior bureaucrats, and an "outsider" who came from "away" laid the foundations for the creation of a network of local bodies to link top-down ventures, and those coming from outside their communities, with initiatives arising from the grassroots. The outsider, who headed the Community Economic Development Division in the Provincial Department of Economic Development and Tourism, had a degree in mathematics. In the 1960s, he decided he would not follow the traditional route of university graduates and go into business or government and pursue a career there. Instead, he joined Canadian University Services Overseas (now CUSO), worked for international development agencies, and then became president of a community college in the Maritimes. While individual effort has had much to do with encouraging community-based development in Nova Scotia, other impersonal forces and factors have played a significant role.

In the 1990s, the province's economy is changing rapidly from an old economy to a new one, from industries built on muscle to those generated by human minds. Coal, steel and shipbuilding are in decline as new technological and service-based ventures generate more and more jobs. Halifax has a large number of software companies; Cape Breton is being described as "Silicon Island East," as a number of media and information technology companies have opened there. Both Halifax and Sydney have casinos, and call centres have been set up in cities and small communities. The province now tends to promote itself as a good place to live and work, rather than relying on financial incentives to lure companies to start new ventures.

In *Making Democracy Work*, Robert Putnam points out the influence of history on how regions develop.[11] In southern Italy, vertical societies prevail. If you want anything, you have to go to the patron, the boss. In northern Italy, people come together formally and informally in mutually beneficial ventures in a horizontal society where there is a great deal of personal interaction in very egalitarian ways.

History, of course, is not destiny. But ingrained habits and history—actual and invented—can play a significant role in helping or hindering social, economic and cultural development. The residents of Cape Breton have developed a very ambivalent attitude towards efforts to order their lives. When the British gained control of the island in 1763, its government tried to stifle coal mining there because it interfered with the home industry. But the prohibition did not stop bootleg mining on Cape Breton. In 1819, 2,000 tons of coal were stolen from the Island. The Duke of York, brother of King George IV, secured a lease on all mineral wealth of Nova Scotia, transferring it—for a share of profits—to his jewellers, who formed the General Mining Association in 1825. This company began mining in the Sydney area in 1827. After its lease was broken in the mid-19th century, others tried to make a fortune by opening coal mines. In 1893, the Boston financier Henry Melville Whitney consolidated the collieries on the eastern side of Sydney Harbour. Whitney further extended his grip on the Island when he established the Dominion Iron and Steel Company in 1898-9.

For the thousands of men and women who left hardscrabble farms in Nova Scotia and their home countries to find work in the mines and mills of the new industrial complexes, "the company" became the central fact in their lives. It employed them, provided houses and stores, and oversaw almost every aspect of their lives. When the mines and the Sydney Steel mill were taken over by the government, dependency was transferred to it.

Private sector ventures have a bottom line. If ventures do not make a profit, they will not survive. Governments have another kind of bottom line—a political one. If they don't do the right sort of things, they will lose votes. Thus millions of dollars have been poured into the old industries (coal and steel) in Nova Scotia, and frantic attempts made to create new ones that will hire hundreds of workers. Meanwhile, little has been done to break the habits of dependency arising from over a century of reliance by Cape Bretoners on "the company" and, then, "the government" to solve the problems of economic development.

Dependency generates two opposite sets of sentiments. If you rely upon a powerful body, then you must not do anything to upset it. When the coal miners of Cape Breton became frustrated with the ways of their employers, they focused their fury on the company stores—the "pluck-me's"—and burned them down. Thus do deference and defiance—sometimes overt, more often covert—emerge from situations of dependency. To assert their identity and integrity, individuals and communities must find ways of subverting, bypassing, undercutting or otherwise neutralizing the damaging ways of the powerful.

In recent years governments seem to have lost their way in regional development. Downsizing, outsourcing, reengineering and other techniques for improving the efficiency of government and giving the private sector freer rein in what once were government preserves have damaged morale in the public sector. The sort of innovation, risk-taking and creativity that marked government policies in community development in the 1960s has vanished.

Despite its vagueness and fuzziness, or perhaps because of these characteristics, community economic development offers an arena for more meaningful and fruitful discussions and for co-operation between government and concerned citizens than was possible in the time of the Culture of Dependency.

During the 1930s, in harder times than our present one, men and women came together to form study clubs and then establish credit unions and co-operatives in Eastern Nova Scotia. The Antigonish Movement, although much mythologized, gave rural people and coal miners more control over their own economic destinies. But the founders of the movement had a long, hard struggle to convince people that they could become masters of their own destiny.[12] Father Jimmy Tompkins, the spiritual father of the Antigonish Movement, arrived in Canso in 1922. Haranguing his parishioners—and anyone else who would listen—Tompkins urged them to learn why they had such miserable lives and what they could do to change them. He helped fishermen to organize, but the trigger for the social movement that he fostered did not occur until 1927. On July 1 in that year, fishermen on the dock at Canso wondered what they had to celebrate on the 60th anniversary of Canadian Confederation. Articulating their discontent, and with help from the Halifax media, these men were able to convince the federal government to launch a Royal Commission on the fisheries of the Maritimes and the Magdalen Islands. Its report, highlighting stories of empty harbours, beached boats and idle men, resonates in our own time as the impact of the closure of the groundfishery becomes increasingly apparent.

There is a tendency, especially in government, to overlook the influence that single individuals and symbolic events can have on the destinies of communities and the shape of the future. Almost 30 years ago, a visiting sociologist from Norway made some astute observations—and sensible recommendations—about the fishing industry in Atlantic Canada. Ottar Brox's study of the Newfoundland fishing industry was subtitled "A Sociology of Economic Dualism."[13] Brox expressed astonishment at the way in which modern methods of fishcatching and processing existed side by side with that he called "medieval" ones. He noted that "The gap between modern and traditional sectors seems to be widening..."[14] In Scandinavia and Iceland, "modernization seems to take place simultaneously in all sectors and regions. Hill farms and isolated villages in Iceland are no less up-to-date than Reykjavik, the capital."[15] Brox saw the "bottleneck factor" in modernizing the fishing industry as cognitive changes. Rather than seeing certain things as constant and unchangeable, all involved in the fishing industry had to see them as variables. He also stressed the need for government policy makers and planners to understand and appreciate how the rural economy works, and the role of non-cash incomes for families in sustaining themselves and their communities. Planners must look at the situation of choice of people in communities, and help them identify ways of enhancing their incomes and strengthening their collective lifestyle through a more rational approach to fishing and local development.

To some extent, this is what The Atlantic Groundfish Strategy (TAGS) sought to do. This strategy, which provided a guaranteed annual income to those who lost their livelihood through the closure of the groundfishery, has largely failed, while dividing communities into "haves" (those who are on TAGS) and "have-nots" (those who qualify for TAGS support.) Some communities, like Isle Madame, have aggressively pursued efforts at economic diversification. Here, one trusted and able individual played a significant role in mobilizing the community and encouraging its members to think about new ways of creating jobs. A survey carried out in Shelburne County in August 1997, however, showed that 91 percent of those in the TAGS programme had made no effort to retrain, find work or start their own ventures. In that county, the

Calmeadow Foundation, a sponsor of community economic development through peer-group lending, has helped some individuals to launch their own businesses.

The establishment of New Dawn, the first community development corporation in Canada, in Sydney in 1973 arose from the frustration of community leaders at the failure of business people from "away" to create viable enterprises. Again and again, Cape Bretoners saw entrepreneurs endowed with government funds set up ventures, and then dismantle them and steal away. One of the founders of New Dawn spoke about the style that the venture adopted to achieve its goal of generating local employment through local effort:

> ...New Dawn asked for government funding for a venture to generate revenue and make some profit in order to buy development land for housing. The program officers said we were not allowed to make money under these programs. We adapted, we became "sea lawyers" clever at finding loopholes...and that's how we kept going...Several times we almost went bankrupt...[16]

That individual credited the volunteer management of New Dawn, all of them local people, for its survival. He echoed a theme that emerges from the world literature on community development: "...[W]hen a group builds up equity, it's independent, and government officials don't like dealing with local groups that have any kind of independence. They normally want the community group to be dependent on the government official for advice and direction...Bureaucracy works that way."[17]

Canadian government, in the past, have often confused development with efforts to control people, especially in marginal regions. If enough jobs can be created, if enough support programmes can be put in place, then social harmony will prevail and conflict be avoided. These development strategies have proved ineffectual. The level of anger is rising in many parts of Canada at the inability and unwillingness of government and the private sector to help people create the good life, with steady jobs, stability and security. More and more individuals, communities and regions believe they are falling into a bottomless void of deprivation and despair.

In *The Ritual Process*, Victor Turner examines what happens to individual communities when their worlds change and they are pushed into limbo.[18] These "liminal entities" and "threshold people" live in an ambiguous world, having slipped or fallen "through the network of classification that normally locate states and positions in cultural space."[19] Bureaucratic societies concerned with the management of members of mass societies operate on the basis of certain categories established in the past to describe groups of individuals.

Community development has often been invoked by governments to bring back neglected minorities into the mainstream of society. Governments tend to reduce it to a series of rituals, procedures and processes that fit bureaucratic imperatives and the categories in current use. So we have aboriginal programmes, women's programmes, projects for the disabled, rather than holistic ones for communities with diverse interests and aspirations. Community development, however, is a form of what Turner calls "anti-structure." Community—a much abused word—comes into being in spaces and places where people feel comfortable with each other. The kitchen meetings and study groups that formed the base units of the Antigonish Movement took place in spaces where community participants felt they could speak openly and freely. MacIntyre has suggested that schools serve as mediating and enabling places in communities where everyone can meet as equals.[20] In schools, those from different sectors of the community can talk, listen, mingle and discuss how best to use resources from inside and outside the community for its benefit.

But moving beyond talk to action requires skilled animators—a word that has recently slipped into the lexicon of community development. In Britain, those dedicated and tough-minded individuals who can bring people and resources together effectively to work for the common good are known as "social entrepreneurs."[21] They use business methods to achieve social goals that neither government nor the private sector can meet. In Canada, the term "community entrepreneur" has emerged to describe those who can generate cohesion among liminal people and motivate and move them towards acting on solutions to their problems, rather than simply lamenting the evils of the world or demanding that the government do something.[22] The pioneers of the Antigonish Movement were among the first to encourage communities to develop their own plans and strategies—"Listen! Study! Discuss! Act!"—for local economic development.

Turner adds a deeper dimension to the usual superficial invocation of "community" and "community development" as panaceas for all the ills of humanity. He prefers the Latin term *communitas* to community to distinguish "this modality of social relationship from an 'area of common living.'"[23] Thus, community is more than a description of people living in one place or sharing one interest. It concerns places where human relationships can be restructured. In these communities, in locations identified as neutral ground, government officials and local residents can meet and talk about ways of working together. Thus those operating from the "top down" will not be required to impose their programmes on communities and individuals who do not fit into them. And people from the grassroots can cease to make demands on government officials that they cannot fulfil.

As Turner puts it, "Liminality implies that the high could not be high unless the low existed, and he who is high must experience what it is like to be low."[24] Turner also cites Martin Buber on community: "Community is the being no longer side by side (and, one might add, above and below) but *with* one another of a multitude of persons. And this multitude, though it moves toward one goal, yet experiences everywhere a turning to, a dynamic facing of, the others, a flowing from *I* to *Thou* . Community is where community happens."[25]

Of Buber's point, Turner says: "Buber lays his finger on the spontaneous, immediate, concrete nature of *communitas*, as opposed to the norm-governed, institutionalized, abstract nature of social structure."[26]

The animator is less the team-leader in the traditional business sense. Rather, he or she resembles an orchestra conductor, ensuring that everyone has the same piece of music in front of them (a concern for creating jobs, an interest in developing a greater degree of local autonomy), assessing the capability of each instrument and its player, and seeking to bring together everyone into a harmonious whole to delight the listeners. This is no task for an amateur. Community development is a window on a wider world, for individuals and collectivities—and a mirror in which they see clearly their deepest fears and limitations, as well as their wildest dreams and aspirations.

Community development involves a shared quest, a voyage on uncharted and dangerous seas in search of those islands of sanity and promise where can be found some answers to enhancing the common good. At base, community development is about the moral, ethical and spiritual concerns that infuse our ideas and condition our actions. In recent years, one of the saner political voices in the world has been Václav Havel, President of the Czech Republic. Branded a public enemy, punished by an authoritarian state that did everything it could to humiliate him and stifle his dissenting voice, Havel became a liminal person. He did not want to hold power, and still prefers to call himself simply "a writer." He has spoken and written on the mystery of the world and of those who live in it:

> In a society which is really alive, there is naturally, always something happening. The interplay of current activities and events, of overt and concealed movement, produces a constant succession of unique situations, which provoke further and fresh movement. The mysterious, vital polarity of the continuous and the changing, the regular and the random, the foreseen and the unexpected, has its effect in the *time dimension* and is borne out in the *flow of events*...wherever there is room for social activity, room is created for a social memory as well. Any society that is alive is a society with a *history*."[27]

Whatever its real or perceived problems, Cape Breton has a history of oppression and dependency, but it has a history too of local initiative and innovation. The Antigonish Movement flowered here, and the community economic development ventures that started with New Dawn have created a history of local achievement through which both local residents and government officials have learned much about working together in mutually beneficial ways. That history, in fact, is a rich and marketable resource. At one time, hundreds of people came to Eastern Nova Scotia to see how residents of small communities organized alternative ways of living and doing business that avoided the excesses of state control and capitalism.

In the 1930s, international communism was promoted by its adherents as the true and only way to utopia. With its failure at the end of the 1980s, international capitalism is being touted as the way to achieve the good society. But the limitations and depredations of private enterprise in the post-communist countries, and those in the developing nations, provide ample evidence of its shortcomings in meeting human needs in human ways. Cape Bretoners have pioneered community economic development—it is lived here, not merely studied and discussed. The Island also has a critical mass of multimedia companies, and access to world-wide information and communication resources. Putting the "clusters" of skilled and knowledgeable people in both fields together could generate material on how communities have used their own resources to gain more control over their lives. Such learning material would find ready markets in both "developed" and "underdeveloped" countries, where communities continue to struggle to make a better life for their residents.

Thus, what has been seen as a constant—Cape Breton as a marginal part of Canada—can be viewed as a variable. In the modern, interconnected global economy, any place can become a centre if it has something to offer that is valued by others seeking to create a better world. Far from being on the edge of Canada, Cape Breton has emerged as a world centre for the study and understanding of community economic development. And through its multimedia companies, it can share its hard-earned knowledge about economic democracy with anyone who has access to even the most elementary forms of electronic communication.

ENDNOTES
1. Letter to the president of the International Society for Community Development in its *Journal* 1(2), July 1966, "Community Development in Canada."
2. For an overview of community development in Canada up to the mid-1970s, see Lotz, Jim, *Understanding Canada.* Toronto: NC Press, 1977.
3. The Economic Council of Canada, *From the Bottom Up: The Community Economic-Development Approach.* Ottawa: Economic Council of Canada, 1990. Shortly after this statement appeared, the Council was abolished by the Federal Government.

4. Michael B. Decter and Jeffrey A. Kowall, *A Case Study of the Kitsaki Development Corporation, La Ronge, Saskatchewan.* Ottawa: Economic Council of Canada, 1989.

5. Elizabeth J. Beale, *Regional Development in Atlantic Canada: An Overview and a Case Study of the Human Resources Development Association.* Ottawa: Economic Council of Canada, 1989.

6. Wayne MacKinnon and Jon Pierce, *The West Prince Industrial Commission: A Case Study.* Ottawa, Economic Council of Canada, 1989.

7. John Wickham, Richard Fuchs and Janet Miller-Pitt, *Where Credit is Due: A Case Study of the Eagle River Credit Union.* Ottawa, Economic Council of Canada, 1989. When a bank refused to establish a branch on Deer Island, New Brunswick in the 1970s, residents formed their own credit union, with the help of a government facilitator.

8. Ralph Matthews, *The Creation of Regional Dependency.* Toronto: University of Toronto Press, 1983, p. 220.

9. Teresa MacNeil, "Assessing the Gap between Community Development Practice and Regional Development Policy," pp. 149-63 in Wharf, Brian and Michael Clague, eds., *Community Organizing: Canadian Experiences.* Toronto: Oxford University Press, 1997.

10. *Ibid.* Deena White, "Contradictory Participation: Reflections on Community Action in Quebec," in Wharf and Clague.

11. Robert D. Putnam, *Making Democracy Work: Civic Traditions in Modern Italy.* Princeton, N.J.: Princeton University Press, 1993.

12. Jim Lotz and Michael Welton, *Father Jimmy: The Life and Times of Father Jimmy Tompkins.* Wreck Cove, Cape Breton: Breton Books, 1997. This book is the first in a series on the Antigonish Movement.

13. Brox, Ottar, *Newfoundland Fishermen in the Age of Industry.* St. John's: Memorial University, Institute of Social and Economic Research, 1972.

14. *Ibid.* p. 6.

15. Ibid.

16. Greg MacLeod, founder of New Dawn, presentation to the Commission of Inquiry on Unemployment Insurance, quoted in its Report, p. 71. This report appeared in 1986.

17. *Ibid.* p. 70. See also Milton J. Esman and Norman T. Uphoff, *Local Organizations: Intermediaries in Rural Development.* Ithaca: Cornell University Press, 1984. As the authors point out, in Kenya and Tanzania, the bureaucracy has "tried to muzzle, if not curtail, self-help organizations because the entire self-help process threatens the bureaucracy's managerial functions, its ideology, and ultimately its means of survival," p. 184.

18. Victor Turner, *The Ritual Process: Structure and Anti-Structure.* Chicago: Aldine, 1969.

19. *Ibid.* p. 95.

20. Gertrude Anne MacIntyre, *Active Partners: Education and Local Development.* Sydney: University College of Cape Breton Press, 1995.

21. Charles Leadbeter, *The Rise of the Social Entrepreneur.* London: Demos, 1997.

22. Jim Lotz, "Community Entrepreneurs," in *Policy Options* , 5 (3), 1984, pp. 40-42.

23. Turner, p. 96.

24. *Ibid.* p. 97.

25. *Ibid.* p. 127.

26. Ibid.

27. Václav Havel, *Living in Truth.* London, Faber and Faber, 1987, p. 25.

Biographies

Keith G. Brown, M.B.A. is Vice-President of Enterprise Cape Breton Corporation. A native of Cape Breton, Keith came to ECBC from the University College of Cape Breton, where he was Dean, Department of Extension and Community Affairs. He is a graduate of St. Francis Xavier University, Antigonish, St. Mary's University in Halifax and City University, Washington, USA. Mr. Brown is also completing doctoral studies in marketing at the University of Bradford in England.

Gary J. Corsano, M.A., LL.B. was born and raised in Sydney, Nova Scotia, where he received his formative education. In 1980, he graduated from Gonzaga University in Spokane, Washington with his Bachelor of Arts Degree in Philosophy and Politics. In 1982, Gary received his Master of Arts Degree from the Politics Department at Dalhousie University. In 1985, he received his Bachelor of Law from the University of New Brunswick. Called to the Bar for the Province of Nova Scotia in 1986, he joined the firm of Sampson McDougall, Sydney, as an associate. He became a partner in 1991.

Constance deRoche, Ph.D. has long been a trend breaker—by migrating *to* Cape Breton and, also, by confining her social anthropological research to North America before it became legitimate to do so. Her early research was comprised of a sociohistorical study of how Acadian villagers adapted to regional economic disparities. More recently, she has studied organizational culture and the mechanisms workers use to deal with bureaucratic change. Since 1973, she has taught anthropology at the University College of Cape Breton.

Michael Gurstein, Ph.D. is ECBC/SSHRC Associate Chair in the Management of Technological Change, Associate Professor of Organizational Management and Founder/Director of the Centre for Community and Enterprise Networking (C\CEN) at University College of Cape Breton. A native of Alberta, he has a Doctorate in Sociology from the University of Cambridge. He owned and co-directed a management consulting company in Ottawa specializing in Information Technology and Organizational Change. Most recently, he worked for the United Nations Secretariat in New York as a Management Advisor.

Harvey Johnstone, Ph.D. is Associate Professor of Business at University College of Cape Breton. His research interests include the potential of small firms to increase net employment, as well as issues associated with firm start-up. Dr. Johnstone has been involved with community economic development corporations, both as a board member and as an advisor, since 1975.

Jim Lotz, M.Sc. is Senior Research Fellow at the Community Economic Development Institute. He first became involved in community economic development in the Yukon Territory in 1960. Since then, he has carried out research, taught, learned, written extensively and been active in this field from Alaska to Slovakia. His experience and ideas are summarized in *The Lichen Factor: The Quest for Community Development in Canada* (UCCB Press, 1998).

Karen Malcolm is a Cape Bretoner and a community activist. She is Development Officer at DIMA (Development Isle Madame Association). In the past five years, she has held various executive positions on the Board of DIMA. She is a past member of the Advisory Board of the CED Institute, University College of Cape Breton.

Scott MacAulay, M.A. is Assistant Professor in the Department of Social Sciences and Practice at the University College of Cape Breton. He has been involved with disability organizations for the last four years and has worked in community economic development for the past 14 years, in Cape Breton, the Northwest Territories, Alberta and British Columbia. He is currently pursuing a Ph.D. at the University of Leeds in England.

Charles MacDonald, Ph.D. has been on the Faculty of the University College of Cape Breton (and its predecessor) since the mid-1960s, teaching Religious Studies. He has been closely associated with the growth of the University College, having a particular interest in bringing its expertise and leadership potential to bear on local problems. He has had long-standing associations with the Mira Pasture Cooperative, New Dawn Enterprises and a variety of cultural and church organizations throughout Cape Breton.

Angus MacIntyre, M.A.E. is a noted trainer and community consultant. He has taught Community Development courses in a First Nations management education programme offered at the University of Manitoba and in an environmental education programme at the Centre for Indigenous Environmental Resources, Winnipeg, Manitoba. He holds a professional designation as an economic developer and is a graduate of the Coady International Institute in Antigonish. Angus received his Masters of Adult Education from St. Francis Xavier University.

Gertrude MacIntyre, Ph.D. is the Founder/Director of the Community Economic Development Institute, and Coordinator of the MBA(CED) programme at the University College of Cape Breton. She has served as Supervisor of Research in the Tompkins Institute, and Chair of the Development Board of BCA Holdings, a community-venture finance company. She is author of *Active Partners: Education and Local Development* (UCCB Press, 1995).

Greg MacLeod, Ph.D. has spent most of his career attempting to bridge the gap between the theory and practice of social-economic change. He studied at the University of Louvain in Belgium, and at Balliol in Oxford. He is now director of the Tompkins Institute at the University College of Cape Breton. He has over 20 years of experience in community economic development in Canada. He is the founding Chairperson of New Dawn Enterprises and of BCA Holdings, a community venture finance company. He is the author of *New Age Business*, and numerous other works on community economic development. In 1997, his most recent book, *From Mondragon to America: Experiments in Community Economic Development*, was published by UCCB Press.

Rankin MacSween, Ed.D. grew up in Ironville, Cape Breton, Nova Scotia. He received his B.A. from St. Francis Xavier University in Antigonish, a Masters degree in counseling and education from the Merill Palmer Institute and a Doctorate in Education from the University of Toronto. He has been associated with New Dawn Enterprises since 1978. In his work with New Dawn, he has been both volunteer and staff member. He served as chair of the social development committee, board member, board chair and executive director. He is now president of New Dawn.

Abstract

Chapter 1

MacIntyre discusses education as the foundation of development and outlines a role for local universities as providers of both theoretical *and* practical support to a region's economic, social and cultural development. She draws on the legacy of Frs. Jimmy Tompkins and Moses Coady to indicate the important role that adult education played in establishing New Dawn Enterprises, the oldest community development corporation in Canada. She points out how the faculty and staff of the University College of Cape Breton (UCCB) were instrumental in providing administrative support, leadership, technical expertise, advocacy skills, resources and access to funding to those involved in New Dawn and other community enterprises such as the Mira Pasture Co-op, a rural agricultural co-operative built on the model of the Common. UCCB helped found the Centre for Community Economic Development to support local ventures. The Centre later became the CED Institute, which founded BCA Holdings Limited, a community-based financial and management company. Community economic development has been the main thrust of the Tompkins and CED Institutes at UCCB, and of the UCCB School of Business, where a Master of Business Administration degree as well as undergraduate courses are offered in the field.

Chapter 2

MacLeod examines the concept of business corporations and suggests they must be redefined to effect change in the social system. It is often large corporations that determine the shape of our society, and at times large firms show little sensitivity to local economies, particularly those in marginal or non-metropolitan regions. MacLeod proposes a new conceptualization of the business corporation. He warns us that while many Westerners rejoiced at the fall of state socialism as a victory for capitalism, capitalistic corporate forms are also deeply flawed. He refers to traditional capitalist leaders who also recognize the dangers of the modern multinationals. Rather than abandon the idea of a large corporation, he calls for a new formulation of the basic idea of a business corporation. His concept of a "community business corporation" is a composite, drawing upon the co-operative tradition as well as that of the modern multi-national. He describes some select examples such as Mondragon in Spain and New Dawn in Cape Breton. These are presented as empirical experiments to test the basic idea: "Can commitment to community serve as a driving force for efficiency and wealth creation, or is egotistical private gain the only adequate motive for business?" He concludes that the answer can only be found in practice.

Chapter 3

Corsano outlines the basic elements of the not-for-profit corporation known as the "community development corporation." He analyzes the legal ramifications of modified corporate structures, compares and contrasts the for-profit with the not-for-profit corporation and examines appropriate incorporating legislation. Some critical reflection is given to the issue of governance in community development corporations, and the problems posed by applying a democratic model to decision-making in that kind of structure.

Chapter 4

The primary purpose of MacSween's chapter is to discuss the critical elements that serve to delineate New Dawn Enterprises Ltd. In other words, the aim is to point to and then examine some of the organization's critical features. To understand New Dawn is to know something about the organization's methodology and the history and culture of the Cape Breton community; it is to know that New Dawn is part of an international movement that may serve to restructure our communities in the 21st century.

Chapter 5

Johnstone outlines the case of BCA Holdings. In virtue of its organizational structure and strategic objectives, BCA Holdings is a unique business entity. However, BCA must find effective ways of dealing with business risk; in this respect, BCA is like any other business venture. Strategies that BCA Holdings uses to manage and reduce risk are discussed.

Chapter 6

MacDonald, in his chapter on the Mira Pasture Co-op, details the attempts of a group of part-time farmers to preserve some elements of farming in communities along the Mira River in Cape Breton. He examines the collaboration of university people with self-employed entrepreneurs and tradespeople, all of whom shared a conviction that rural values can be preserved by fostering rural activities. His essay presents a case study of the basic principles of CED: the importance of collaboration with elected officials, the critical role of "sweat equity," the importance of community support, the innovative development of capital resources, and the necessity to tailor projects to changing circumstances.

Chapter 7

The collapse of the groundfish strategy confronted Isle Madame with a serious economic situation, including the loss of 500 jobs. In 1993, with support from Human Resources Development Canada and funding through the Community Futures programme, a community economic development strategy was set up to develop action plans that could be widely supported by the community, but tied to specific development projects and opportunities. Development Isle Madame

(DIMA) was established as a community-owned, non-profit limited company, dedicated to fostering the necessary social and economic changes on Isle Madame to ensure its future. Its primary goal was to help create long-term, sustainable jobs for the residents of Isle Madame. To accomplish this goal, DIMA provided a venue for local community leaders to contribute to the economic development process, and to assist in developing infrastructure to support economic development on Isle Madame. It rested firmly on the commitment of local people, many of whom are not necessarily professionals, but all of whom have a genuine interest in preserving and developing the community. It has been a long process of self-education to determine what is needed for local development: writing proposals, seeking funds, developing community strategies, and motivating people to learn.

Chapter 8

Brown reflects on the policies of Enterprise Cape Breton Corporation (ECBC) that have supported CED. Two initiatives of the Corporation that have had varying degrees of success, tourism and aquaculture, are explored. The Chapter then turns to the Corporation's *raison d'être*. Its 30-year developmental strategies are explored, and the author comments on other federal initiatives for economic development on Cape Breton Island.

Chapter 9

Gurstein provides a broad framework for understanding certain limitations on the development of Information and Communications Technology (ICT) for local community development. The development of local economies takes place within the globalization of the world economy. Globalization is being propelled, in part, by ICT and may be eroding the economic base of some local communities. But it also provides new opportunities for local communities to change the conditions of their participation in the national and international marketplace. New and valuable opportunities for information-intensive work are emerging. Presently, the province of Nova Scotia is a pioneer in the use of technology to advance local development. A number of public and private organizations are involved in this effort.

Chapter 10

MacAulay tells the story of the successful efforts of Cape Breton's largest organization of persons with disabilities to establish a Centre of Excellence to provide service in technology and entrepreneuring. This group engaged in a long process of strategic planning and forming partnerships with public and private institutions to bring the project to fruition. That process is described in detail.

Chapter 11

As community economic development or "CED" becomes an increasingly popular term, we should query its meanings. Instead of prescribing the essence of what CED is or should be, this chapter takes a phenomenological approach to the quest. That is, deRoche works at discovering what CED's proponents think it is, as expressed in their statements and practice. She surveys and compares usages in order to raise questions and generate debate about the role of community, local ownership, and locus of control. The author concludes that Fontan's distinction between liberal and progressive practice is better seen as part of a continuum that extends to a radical end-point. If CED is essentially a set of renewal strategies for coping with global restructuring, its hope lies in debate, analysis, and on-going experimentation.

Chapter 12

In his chapter, MacIntyre compiles informal research by asking timely, probing questions about jobs. In his quest for answers, his research techniques were heavily influenced by Patton's three works on qualitative research methodology. He also surveyed the kinds of employment his research subjects preferred. His informal research project signals the need for a more extensive, formal investigation in this area.

Chapter 13

Lotz relates community development to liminality, the state of being betwixt and between old ways and new demands. As he points out, community development, in all of its various forms, has usually been invoked by governments as a way of handling social and economic tension in marginal regions. Interest in community economic development has risen in Canada, as the traditional "top down" ways of creating employment have faltered. As more and more people in marginal areas fall into a state of limbo, it is necessary to identify places and spaces where concerned citizens and government officials can meet and interact in mutually beneficial ways. Meetings in such places, and action based on what is decided there, require the services of skilled animators and community entrepreneurs. The skills and experience gained in community economic development in Cape Breton, a pioneer area in the field, is making the Island a centre of knowledge about this process. This knowledge can be used effectively to generate jobs and local identity. Thus, far from being a marginal part of Canada, Cape Breton has emerged as a world centre in this field. What has been learned here is of wide interest and could be marketed, using modern communications and information technology, all over the world.

BIBLIOGRAPHY

Acheson, T.W. "The National Policy and the Industrialisation of the Maritimes, 1880-1990." In P. Bucker and D. Frank, eds. *The Acadiensis Reader, Volume 2: Atlantic Canada After Confederation*. Fredericton: Acadiensis Press, 1985.

Banfield, E. *The Moral Basis of a Backward Society*. New York: The Free Press, 1958.

Beale, Elizabeth J. *Regional Development in Atlantic Canada: An Overview and a Case Study of the Human Resources Development Association*. Ottawa: Economic Council of Canada, 1989.

Berger, Peter and Richard Neuhaus. *To Empower People: The Role of Mediating Structures in Public Policy*. Washington: American Institute for Public Policy Research, 1977.

Bevan, Julie. "Barriers to Business Start-Up: A Study of the Flow Into and Out of Self-Employment." Research Paper No. 71, Department of Employment, HMSO, United Kingdom, 1989.

Bickerton, J. *Nova Scotia, Ottawa and the Politics of Regional Development*. Toronto: University of Toronto Press, 1990.

Birch, D. *The Job Generation Process*. Cambridge, MA: Massachusetts Institute of Technology Program on Neighbourhood and Regional Change, 1979.

-----*Job Creation in America: How Our Smallest Companies Put The Most People To Work*. New York: The Free Press, 1987.

Brait, A.A. "From Dependence to Enterprise: Report of the Enterprise Cape Breton Assessment Team." Prepared for the Minister Responsible for the Atlantic Canada Opportunities Agency. Halifax, 1991.

Brox, Ottar. *Newfoundland Fishermen in the Age of Industry.* St. John's: Memorial University, Institute of Social and Economic Research, 1972.

Bryant, Christopher. "The Locational Dynamics of Community Economic Development." In David J.A. Douglas, ed., *Community Economic Development in Canada*, Vol. 1, edited by David J.A. Douglas. Toronto: McGraw-Hill Ryerson, 1994, pp. 203-236.

Calouste Gulbenkian Foundation. *Community Business Works.* London: Gulbenkian Foundation, UK Branch, 1982.

Cameron, Silver Donald. "Whither UCCB? A Certain Degree of Difference." In *New Maritimes*, November/December 1995, p. 5.

Christenson, James A. and Jerry W. Robinson, Jr. *Community Development in America.* Ames, Iowa: The Iowa State University, 1980.

Coady, Moses. *Masters of Their Own Destiny.* New York: Harper and Row, 1939.

Davis, Charles H. "Integración económica de América del Norte y la política de innovación en Canada." pp. 105-150 in *Ciencia y Tecnología, y Tratado de Libre Comercio.* Consejo Consultivo de Ciencias, Presidencia de la República/SECOFI, Mexico, 1993.

-----"Innovation Support Services for Innovative Communities." In D. Bruce and M. Whitlaw, eds., *Community-Based Approaches to Rural Development.* Sackville, New Brunswick: Mount Allison University Press, 1997.

Davies, A. "A Prairie Dust Devil: The Rise and Decline of a Research Institute." In *Human Organization*, Vol. 20(1), 1968, pp. 56-63.

Decter, Michael and Jeffrey A. Kowall. *A Case Study of the Kitsaki Development Corporation, La Ronge, Saskatchewan.* Ottawa: Economic Council of Canada, 1989.

deRoche, Constance P., comp. *Entrepreneurial Resource Guide.* Sydney: Community Economic Development Institute, 1998 (forthcoming).

-----*The Village, The Vertex: Adaptation to Regionalism and Development in a Complex Society.* Occasional Papers in Anthropology, 12. Halifax: Department of Anthropology, St. Mary's University, 1985.

deRoche, Constance P., and John E. deRoche, eds. *"A Rock in a Stream": Living with the Political Economy of Underdevelopment in Cape Breton.* Research and Policy Papers 7. St. John's: Institute of Social and Economic Research, Memorial University of Newfoundland, 1987.

De Toqueville, Alexis. *Democracy in America.* New York: The New America Library, 1956.

Dienes, Bruce. *A Summary Report on Wire Nova Scotia, 1997.* N.d., C/CEN Occasional Paper 3.

Donald, J.R. *The Cape Breton Coal Problem.* Montréal: 1966.

Douglas, David J.A., ed. *Community Economic Development in Canada, Vol. 2.* Toronto: McGraw-Hill Ryerson, 1995.

-----*Community Economic Development in Canada, Vol. 1.* Toronto: McGraw-Hill Ryerson, 1994."Context and Conditions of Community Economic Development in Canada: Governmental Institutional Responses." in *Community Economic Development in Canada*, Vol. 1, edited by David J.A. Douglas. Toronto: McGraw-Hill Ryerson, 1994b, pp. 65-118.

-----"Community Economic Development in Canada: Issues, Scope, Definitions and Directions." in *Community Economic Development in Canada, Vol. 1*, edited by David J.A. Douglas. Toronto: McGraw-Hill Ryerson, 1994a, pp. 1-64.

-----*Community Economic Development and You*. Ottawa: Employment and Immigration Canada, 1992.

Drucker, P. *Post-Capitalist Society*. New York: Harper-Collins, 1993.

Economic Council of Canada. *From the Bottom Up: The Community Economic Development Approach*. Ottawa: Economic Council of Canada, 1989.

The Economist, "Shop of Little Horrors," Nov. 13, 1993.

Esman, Milton J. and Norman T. Uphoff. *Local Organizations: Intermediaries in Rural Development*. Ithaca, NY: Cornell University Press, 1984.

Fairbairn, Brett et al., eds. *Co-operatives & Community Development: Economics in Social Perspective*. Saskatoon: Centre for the Study of Co-operatives, University of Saskatchewan, 1995.

Fitzpatrick, Joey. "Taking Charge." *Nova Scotia: Open to the World* (July) 1997:2 6.

Fontan, Jean-Marc. *A Critical Review of Canadian, American, & European Community Economic Development Literature*. Vancouver: CCE/Westcoast Publications, 1993.

Friedman, Milton. *Free to Choose*. New York: Harcourt Brace, 1980.

Gasse, Yvonne. "Importance of the Small and Medium-sized Enterprise in the Canadian Economy." In *Journal of Small Business and Entrepreneurship*, Vol. 11(3), 1994.

Gates, William. *The Road Ahead.* New York: Viking Press, 1995.

Goodpaster, Kenneth. "Can a Corporation Have a Conscience?" In *Harvard Business Review*, January-February 1982.

Government of Manitoba. *A Study of the Population of Indian Ancestry Living in Manitoba.* Winnipeg:Department of Agriculture and Immigration, 1959, p. 109.

Gower, L.C.B. *The Principles of Modern Company Law.* London: Stevens and Sons, 1969.

Greider, William. *One World, Ready or Not: The Manic Logic of Global Capitalism,* New York: Simon and Schuster, 1997.

Gunn, Christopher, and Hazel Dayton Gunn. *Reclaiming Capital: Democratic Initiative and Community Development.* Ithaca: Cornell University Press, 1991.

Gurstein, Michael. "Managing Technology for Non-Metropolitan Development: A Case Study of Cape Breton Island," UNIG Conference Proceedings, UNESCO Conference on Management of Technology. Istanbul, Turkey, 1996.

--- *Applying the Concept of Flexible Networks to Community Access Computing.* n.d., ms.

Gurstein, Michael and Kristin Andrews. *A Summary Report on Wire Nova Scotia 1996.* N.d., C/CEN Occasional Paper 2.

Hauben, Michael and Ronda. *Netizens: On the History and Impact of Usenet and the Internet.* Los Almitos, CA: EEE Computer Society, 1997.

Havel, Václav. *Living in Truth.* London: Faber and Faber, 1987.

House, Douglas. *Building on our Strengths: The Report of the Royal Commission on Employment and Unemployment.* St. John's: The Queen's Printer, 1986.

-----"Rural Development and Technological Change," pp. 61-69 in *Changing Newfoundland's Economy Through Science and Technology. Seminar Proceedings.* Newfoundland and Labrador Science and Technology Advisory Council and Economic Council of Newfoundland and Labrador, St. John's, 1991.

Jacobs, Jane. *Cities and the Wealth of Nations: Principles of Economic Life.* New York: Random House, 1984.

Korten, David. *When Corporations Rule the World.* West Hartford, CT: Kumarian Press/Berrett-Koehler Publishers, 1995.

Lagassé, Jean. "Community Development in Manitoba." In *Human Organization*, 20(4), Winter 1961-2, p. 234.

Laidlaw, Alexander. Outline of an Address presented to a Community Development Workshop for the Atlantic Provinces, Wolfville, Nova Scotia, January 29, 1975.

-----In *The Atlantic Co-operator*, December 1980.

Leadbeter, Charles. *The Rise of the Social Entrepreneur.* London: Demos, 1997.

Lerner, Sally et. al. *An Evaluation of Wire Nova Scotia 1996.* N.d., C/CEN Occasional Paper 1.

Lewellen, Ted C. *Dependency and Development: An Introduction to the Third World.* Westport, CT: Bergin & Garvey, 1995.

Lotz, Jim. "Community Entrepreneurs." In *Policy Options*, Vol. 5(3), 1984.

-----*Understanding Canada.* Toronto: NC Press, 1994.

-----"The Beginning of Community Development in English-Speaking Canada." In Wharf and Clague, eds., 1997.

Lotz, Jim and Pat Lotz. *Cape Breton Island*. Vancouver: Douglas, David and Charles, 1974.

Lotz, Jim and Michael Welton. *Father Jimmy: The Life and Times of Father Jimmy Tompkins.* Wreck Cove, Cape Breton: Breton Books, 1997.

Lynch, Allan. "As Good as Gold." *Nova Scotia: Open to the World.* July 1997:11-14.

Mander, Jerry and Edward Goldsmith, eds. *The Case Against the Global Economy.* San Francisco: Sierra Club Books, 1996.

Mason, Colin and Richard Harrison. "Strategies for Expanding the Informal Venture Capital Market." In *International Small Business Journal,* Vol. 2, No. 4, 1993.

-----"Closing the Regional Equity Gap: The Role of Informal Venture Capital." In *Small Business Economics,* Vol. 7, No. 2, 1995.

Matthews, Ralph. *The Creation of Regional Dependency.* Toronto: University of Toronto Press, 1983.

MacAulay, Scott. *Look to the Future: Five Year Strategic Plan.* Sydney: Community Involvement of the Disabled, 1995.

MacIntyre, Gertrude Anne. *Active Partners: Education and Local Development.* Sydney: University College of Cape Breton Press, 1995.

MacKinnon, Wayne and Jon Pierce. *The West Prince Industrial Commission: A Case Study.* Ottawa: Economic Council of Canada, 1989.

MacLeod, Greg. *New Age Business*. Ottawa: The Canadian Council on Social Development, 1986.

-----Presentation to the Commission of Inquiry on Unemployment Insurance, 1986.

-----"Community Business: A Video/Booklet Series." Tompkins Institute/University College of Cape Breton, Sydney, Nova Scotia.

-----*The Concept in Operation.* Sydney: Tompkins Institute, University College of Cape Breton, 1991a.

-----*New Dawn Enterprises.* Sydney: Tompkins Institute, University College of Cape Breton, 1991b.

-----"Atlantic Canadian Roots." Ch. 2 in *Community Economic Development in Canada.* David Douglas, ed., Toronto: McGraw-Hill, 1995.

-----*"The Knowledge Economy and the Social Economy: University Support for Community Enterprise Development as a Strategy for Economic Regeneration in Distressed Regions in Canada and Mexico."* Triple Helix Conference, University of Amsterdam, The Netherlands, Jan. 3, 1996.

-----*From Mondragon to America: Experiments in Community Economic Development.* University College of Cape Breton Press, 1997.

MacNeil, Teresa. "Assessing the Gap between Community Development Practice and Regional Development Policy." In Wharf, Brian and Michael Clague, eds.

MacSween, J. Rankin. "New Dawn Enterprises Ltd.: A Community Economic Development Experiment." Pp. 182-191 in *Community Economic Development: In Search of Empowerment*, 2nd ed., edited by Eric Shragge. Montréal: Black Rose Books, 1997.

-----*The Values Underlying a Community Development Corporation.* Ph.D. Dissertation, Department of Education, University of Toronto, 1994.

Newman, Peter C. *Company of Adventurers*. Markham, Ontario: Viking/Penguin Books, 1985.

Nozick, Marcia. *No Place Like Home: Building Sustainable Communities*. Ottawa: Canadian Council on Social Development, 1992.

Oliver, Michael. *The Politics of Disablement*. London: MacMillan Press Ltd., 1990.

-----"The Disability Movement is a New Social Movement." In *Community Development Journal,* Vol. 32, No.3, 1997.

Oliver, Michael and Colin Barnes. "Discrimination, disability and welfare: From needs to rights." In *Disabling Barriers – Enabling Environments*, John Swain, Vic Finklestein et al., eds. London: SAGE Publications, 1996.

O'Neil, Tim. *From the Bottom Up: The Community Economic Development Approach*. Ottawa: Economic Council of Canada, 1990.

Patton, Michael Quinn. *Qualitative Evaluation Methods*. Beverly Hills, CA: SAGE Publications, 1980.

-----*Practical Evaluation*. Beverly Hills, CA: SAGE Publications, 1982.

-----*Utilization - Focused Evaluation*. Beverly Hills, CA: SAGE Publications, 1986.

Perry, S. *Communities on the Way: Rebuilding Local Economies in the United States and Canada*. Albany, NY: State University of New York Press, 1997.

Plunkett Foundation. *Yearbook of Co-operative Enterprise*. Oxford, UK: 1992.

Porter, Michael E. *The Competitive Advantage of Nations*. Boston: Harvard College, 1993.

Putnam, Robert D. *Making Democracy Work: Civic Traditions in Modern Italy.* Princeton, NJ: Princeton University Press, 1993.

Quarter, Jack. *Canada's Social Economy: Co-operatives, Non-profits, and Other Community Enterprises.* Toronto: James Lorimer & Company, 1992.

Reich, Robert B. *The Work of Nations.* Vintage Books, Random House, New York, 1982.

Rosner, Menachem. "Worker Ownership, Ideology and Social Structure in 'Third-Way' Work Organizations." In *Economic and Industrial Democracy* 12(3), 369-384.

Roulstone, Alan. "Access to new technology in the employment of disabled people." In Swain and Finklestein, eds.

Rutherford, Jonathon, ed. *Identity: Community, Culture and Difference.* London: Lawrence and Wishart, 1990.

Shragge, Eric, ed. *Community Economic Development: In Search of Empowerment*, 2nd ed. Montréal: Black Rose Books, 1997.

Schratz, Michael and Rob Walker. *Research as Social Change: New Opportunities for Qualitative Research.* London and New York: Routledge, 1995.

Schuler, Douglas. *New Community Networks: Wired for Change.* New York: Addison-Wesley, 1995.

Sinclair, Peter. "Underdevelopment and Regional Inequality." Pp. 358-376 in *Social Issues and Contradictions in Canadian Society,* edited by B. Singh Bolaria. Toronto: Harcourt Brace Jovanovich, Canada, 1991.

Small, Doug. "Fresh Start for Cape Breton." *Reader's Digest,* February 1997: 61-65.

Storey, D.J. and S.G. Johnson. *Job Creation in Small and Medium-Sized Enterprises: Commission of the European Communities, Vol.1.* Newcastle, UK: Centre for Urban and Regional Development Studies, University of Newcastle-Upon-Tyne, 1987.

Swain, John, Vic Finklestein et al., eds. *Disabling Barriers – Enabling Environments.* London: SAGE Publications, 1996.

Tompkins, Rev. Dr. James. *Knowledge for the People: A Call to St. Francis Xavier's College*: Antigonish: St. F.X. University, 1921.

Turner, Victor. *The Ritual Process: Structure and Anti-Structure.* Chicago: Aldine, 1969.

Wharf, Brian and Michael Clague, eds. *Community Organizing: Canadian Experiences.* Toronto: Oxford University Press, 1997.

White, Deena. "Contradictory Participation: Reflections on Community Action in Quebec," in Wharf and Clague, eds.

Wickham, John, Richard Fuchs and Janet Miller-Pitt. *Where Credit is Due: A Case Study of the Eagle River Credit Union.* Ottawa: Economic Council of Canada, 1989.